Successology

The Science of Success

AN XOLOGY GUIDE

Written by
Scott

Published by
1stCo Books

Copyright & Reproduction Information

Successology:

The Science of Success

Written by
Scott Rogers

Editor
Mindy Brodhead Averitt

Graphic Design
Mathew Hodgkinson

Additional Content
Janice Sommerville

Table of Contents

Part Two - The Projected You

Xology - Symbol Guide

Through this and other **Xology Guides** you will find an array of symbols that identify passages and points as being of particular interest (or dis-interest - this being the point of the symbols for you).

Quote
A quote, strangely enough

Web Link
*Related or supplemental information can be found at indicated website or at **www.Xology.com***

Gospel
This information is given according to the gospel of Scott

(Bloody Stupid!)
Stay away from this! Indicates misconceptions and lies

Tools
This passage mentions business or life 'tools' available to you

Target
Make note of these targets. They are tasks and objectives for you to complete

Instant Return
Look out for this symbol for advice that yields a quick return and improvement

Nota Bene (mark well)
Important stuff. Read this care-fully, then read it once more

Statistics
Facts, figures, studies, charts and graphs

Dedication

This guide is dedicated to my daughter, Kimberley, and to the many who have inspired me and helped shape this future for me. Thank you.

Acknowledgements

I would like to acknowledge the people who have helped to research, compile, check, proof, design, market, edit, add to, delete from, inspire, and complete so many other important tasks. Special thanks go to Mathew, Stuart, and Angie.

Appreciation to the many people who have contributed to my development and success: Leo, Wendy, Edith, Stacey, Rachel, Helen, Petriz, Liam, Lisa, Dianne, Mindy, Janet, Sheri, Dana, Mimi, Pat, Janice, Dale, Amy, Chuck, Jeff, Marc, Ray, Cathy, Mandie, John, Ron, Jason, Myrtle, Charlie, Beverly, BJ, Britt, Homer, Linda, Jenny, Lisa, Randy, Andrea, Kay, Sarah, Suzanne, Mary, Teresa, Randy, Michelle, Tony, Kelly, Matt, Calvin, Karen, Gavin, Celeste, Jerry, Natasha, Wesley, Fran, Albert, Tim, Christine, Julie, Flo, Celia, David, Kevin, Sylvia, Bonita, Atrayee, Naresh, Jay, Louise, Ann, David, Bibi, Bella, Emma, Cheryl, Barbara, Susan, Steve, Nick, Howard...and those who I have inadvertently forgotten.

And those who have inspired me in other ways: Graham, Linda, Allan, Tina, Lisa, Kathy, Roy, Chris, Anne, John, Lionel, Sarah, Sue, Emma, Ruth, Jonathan, Gilda, Daryl, Keith, Carlos, Louis, Daniel, Martin, Jo, Sue, Terri, Spencer, Susan, Val, Shirley, Dawn, Dave... and those who continue to do so.

And the many fascinating and brilliant clients that I have had the opportunity to work with worldwide, and continue to work with - and by whom I am continuously inspired, as I attempt to inspire.

Successology

The Science of Success

*Your success starts
right this way...*

Preface

I. A Bit of History

Since the birth of mankind (don't groan - I'll leave out the Stone Age), there has been a social hierarchy in place, a comparison of individual strengths within social gatherings. The strongest would demand the best food, the best shelter, and the best treatment. Maybe this was the first form of success? The weaker members of the prehistoric society could only look on meekly wishing and wondering why it was not them. Nothing much has changed since then you say?

"History is more or less bunk! It's tradition. We don't want tradition. We want to live in the present and the only history that is worth a tinker's damn is the history we make today."
Henry Ford (1863 - 1947)

Offspring would soon recognize that the strongest could command the best for themselves and leave the rest to the weakest. And thus began the instinctive race for the survival of the fittest. Success was measured as a sign of strength and muscles.

As society developed a more complex hierarchy also developed. Soon it was not merely the strongest in battle that would reign supreme. Success came to those with the best and most powerful allies, through strength in numbers and of group, and through strength of birthrights rather than the physical strength of the individual.

Generations arose where those born to nothing could rise through the ranks and realize a broader potential. Soon (and more recently) came the realization that all men were born equal. Well perhaps not equal, but with the equal ability to become equal - something far more important and valuable. This premise should be at the center of our motivations, that we are able to succeed and attain any kind of success. This should spur us on at all times. You can be or achieve anything - nothing is impossible.

II. Equal Odds

The questions of why we are here on Earth, why some have more than others, why we feel a sense of inadequacy, and a sense of lack of fulfillment are more prevalent now then ever. Have you, like me, ever laid in bed at night wondering about it all?

"Let us be moral. Let us contemplate existence."
Charles Dickens (1812 - 1870)

Successology attempts to answer such questions (and more) and opens the doors to everyone who reads these pages (I don't have a preference to your social, economic or ethnic status). This book should be considered a tool, or a combination to a hefty safe inside of which are subtle and powerful treasures which will give you more control. Successology will help you find and attain personal success in your life.

Successology on its own will not magically put you at your destination on some fantastical flying carpet, but it will help you to get to where you want to go. You are the vehicle to your own success. This book provides a clearly defined set of ideas, suggestions, tips, and ethics to apply in a personal and individual way to you.

Too often, we are offered the "perfect" solution to all our problems. "Lose all that weight you put on over the last year in just a few days!" Rubbish!!! "Use our program, and you will be rich quick!!!" Hogwash!!! Quick fixes are like drug fixes: After the euphoria comes a crashing down to reality. Perhaps if we were machines, such offerings might work. This book is different. Successology assumes that:

The reader is a person (with us so far?)
An individual   (not just one of the crowd)
A unique human being with personalized desires and aspirations.

(If any of the three descriptions above do not apply to you, please carefully place this book back on the shelf from whence it came, and slowly move away from Successology.)

III. The Successology Difference

I am not attempting to change you (the reader) into something you are not - how could I, or how could anyone? I am sure you've seen the books, the tapes, and seminars - "become more assertive / powerful / charismatic / persuasive / expressive" etc. etc. Maybe, as I have, you have entertained the idea that some of these claims could be true (or was it that we wanted them to be true?). And, after paying for the seminar, kits, guides, and matching pens, we felt cheated or like failures when they didn't work; maybe they did work and elevated us for a while but then it all faded and was forgotten about too soon.

Successology is different (yet effective) because it will open your eyes to your own true potential. This book will unlock some of those hidden doors inside of you.

 "I consider a human soul without education like a marble in a quarry, which shows none of its inherent beauties until the skill of the polisher sketches out the colors, makes the surface shine and discovers every ornamental cloud, spot, and vein which runs through it."
Joseph Addison (1672 - 1719)

More than likely the skills that you currently possess and carry through your day, those skills within you right now (as you read these pages) are more or less your lot for life. If this is the case, then why should you bother to continue with this book, or with life for that matter? If what you have now in the way of skill sets is complete, then what is the point? Well, imagine your skills are seeds. In the palm of your hand, they look pretty insignificant, don't they? Now imagine that you plant them, nurture them, care and tend for them. What will you have? A huge field to harvest. Your reward will be great. This is my aim, to assist you in planting your skills, to help you nurture them into a huge harvest of success. Pretty exciting stuff, eh?

IV. Making it Stick

But you and I know that any change in you is only permanent when your whole self is behind it. If you've ever tried to quit smoking (or the dreaded dieting) you'll know that it won't work unless you really, really want it to. Deep character and personality changes are rarely ever seen. The few occasions when people undergo a radical change in a short period of time usually stem from major events: life-threatening situations, the death of loved ones, or betrayal etc.   Assuming that no one wants to go through these terrible things in the hope of finding positive growth, we are left with working with what we have at the moment.

Making changes in the way that we use, show, and recognize our existing core abilities and stronger facets can facilitate changes in our careers and personal lives. That's what I am going to do right now with you. Excited yet?

I would like to offer you an opportunity to adapt, improve, develop, and diversify your talents; and then more importantly, learn how your talents are best applied and portrayed. Part One of this book, entitled The Real You, explains the basis of this phenomenon. You are about to embark on an exciting journey. Success is not some elusive mountain you cannot climb.

Successology will have immediate results in certain areas of your life; however, claiming that an all-encompassing change will take place by merely reading this book is ridiculous. While certain areas can be adapted and results may be phenomenal, a change in attitude, a change in habits and a change in lifestyle are not so easy and quick to attain. It has taken you years to get to this stage in your life. For each year a bad habit has been in place in your life, it will take a month to overcome it fully. So please bear with me; I will be here (hopefully) in the coming months to see your full development (God willing).

"Men's natures are alike; it is their habits that carry them far apart."
Confucius (551 - 479 BC)

V. Red Light? Green Light!

I often hear from many of my clients how happy they are with their progress. However, even during their happy and positive feedback, I constantly remind them that on all journeys, you have to expect some red lights, some stop signs, occasional rest room breaks and even a flat tire. You must accept this, too. Let's get real here; we are talking about your life and your success. As with any good meal, it tastes much better when it is properly prepared and when it is given time. So, with this in mind, let's spend time on you together, and let's move on.

"An obstacle is something you see when you take your eyes off your goal."
Anon

VI. Plot a Course & Schedule

You may think that this is just a book (well it is made of paper and bought from a book store; however, let's use our imagination here), but I want you to imagine Successology is really your personal life coach, or a genie trapped in these covers and filled with resources, guidance, and even perhaps personal wishes. One such resource for you to take full advantage of is the **Xology.com Success Schedule**. *Visit the website and sign up for your own custom and private schedule to track and encourage you.*

www.Xology.com
- Your helpful site

By implementing and adhering to a schedule, you will be assured that your full potential has a greater chance of being reached and that your goal of success has real hope of being attained.

Successology will cover topics that may reach into the very essence of who you are. I make no apologies for the depth I ask you to reach, nor do I make any apologies for the probing nature of the questions I ask (or that I suggest you ask yourself). However, the depths you reach will be reflected in the heights you attain following your involvement in these pages.

> *"The tragedy of life doesn't lie in not reaching your goal. The tragedy lies in having no goals to reach."*
> **Benjamin E. Mays (1895 - 1984)**

VII. The Successful You

The purpose of Successology is to allow you to recognize the potential success you carry within yourself and to teach you how to harness that very success to advance your life in positive directions.

Success is like a kinetic force that, once started, moves all actions and drives our lives to completeness. For years, philosophy has dealt with the question of what makes man complete, and though this question has never been fully answered, the common thread of intellectual thought throughout history is that man cannot help but search for an ideal form of happiness.

Successology, in large part, provides a means for the

achievement of your happiness, but by no means is this book a comprehensive text. In as much as I would love to be your oracle (though many might describe me as an orifice) and provide you with a fabulous future, answering all your questions, and predicting your life for you, I visualize the purpose of this book to be a means for a progressive change and re-evaluation of your life, or to put it another way, a thought-provocative element you introduce into your life to find your real success.

This text will cause you to examine your life, and the **Xology** website will further this process by allowing you to monitor the changes that occur as you follow and immerse yourself into Successology. I am in the business of helping you learn to find the diamonds within you and eliminating all the superfluous sand in your life. This book will cover with you the following questions:

> -Who are you?
> -What is success?
> -How can you achieve success?

I will help you provide and fulfill the answers.

VIII. Roots of Success

To understand the definition of success, we must first look towards its roots. Perhaps the first understanding of success can be derived from Grecian history and the teachings of Plato and Aristotle.

 "We are made with all the tools we need. Life in this sense is moving towards completeness."
Aristotle (384 - 322 B.C.)

Plato taught of moving the soul towards an emulation of an

ideal that in so doing would make the soul healthy. This state of good health was thought to be obtainable through an understanding that the soul could not attain perfection. Instead, such health could only be found in the acknowledgement of a quest – the journey of the soul toward divinity. In this sense, success could be thought of as the fuel that powers your vehicle on this journey, or your driving force that continually draws you towards a state of good soul health.

"In imperfection we find perfection."
Milton (1608 - 1674)

While considering the intangibility of success we should understand that with each step towards it, we obtain a small part of it. The incomplete achievement in itself then becomes a driving force.

As Aristotle suggested, we are all born with the characteristics necessary for a successful life. Such a gift of nature suggests that simply living is moving towards perfection (wouldn't that be nice!). Sadly, perfection in the hands of man takes effort.

Several factors are necessary in order to nurture the gifts with which we are born, perhaps the most important gift being purpose. Your purpose gives you a map that will take you from where you are now to your end goal – a very definite path that you will follow to reach your destination. Have you ever tried to take a big road trip without planning a route in advance? Well, my advice is don't, it is awful. Planning is also needed to arrive at your goals in life. Your destination may even change en route. Be prepared.

On this journey, your actions must be examined and ques-

tioned. "Why did I do that?" "Why am I going to do this?" "Is this action taking me closer to an end purpose?" Purpose is crucial in crafting the completeness you hope to achieve.

Consider success as being the goal that will enable you to sharpen your awareness of your actions. This will allow you more control over your end. With control you find balance: and in balance you find peace, clarity, and direction.

IX. The Successology Philosophy

Our bodies are machines run by the forces around us. Depending on how we live our lives, we can change the natural chain of events and utilize them to attain a higher and more profitable end.

When we are born, I believe that we are given a few chosen talents. If we recognize those talents and use them in our day-to-day lives, we will ultimately gain personal success. To be successful, we must first consider what we define as success. What in your eyes makes a successful person? Is it money, a stable job, happiness, family, a legacy to leave behind?

I believe that success is finding balance and peace within yourself; in essence, being happy. Money, nice possessions, job satisfaction (things I personally enjoy, like and strive to attain), and all those things that we generally associate with success are actually merely the tools or the stepping-stones to our ultimate goal. After all, looking successful and having the objects of success around you does not make a person truly so.

If you enjoy a little science, then you will be pleased to know that I like to compare the talents we are given to a scientific theory: kinetic and potential energy. Newton denotes that potential energy is stored and on its release becomes kinetic. Kinetic energy is an on-going force that, once started, may never stop; it may even grow or expand.

Remember those awful executive desk toys with the swinging metal balls in the cradle? They are called Newton's cradles and work when one ball strikes another causing that ball to strike another ball and so forth. Once started, its own force keeps the balls in motion.

If you apply this physics to your own life, you too have talents that are suppressed, hidden, and unknown. Once unleashed, these talents can bring you the fulfillment and success you only dreamed about. You can turn one kind of energy into another.

Whilst my physics may seem crude, I believe that success works in a manner similar to what Newton described. The degree of success you have rests in your ability to move from the potential of success (something everyone holds within them) within the field of force (the world), to a state of kinetic motion. This is very much like Newton's cradle. Once you are charged with the desire to gain success in your life, a chain reaction then occurs.

Success is not a state of tangible being; it is a state of mind and purpose.

Success is not merely the illusion of success, but instead the actual motion of being successful, which you can only achieve by jump-starting with success-motion. I am confident that Successology will provide that start for you.

Part One

The Real You

Overview
In this part

Introduction
You Are Not Unique
Overview Of The Three You's concept
Summary Of Introduction

Element One
The Real You
The Kitchens Of Our Mind
Tips
Summary Of Element One

Element Two
Who Knows You best
Why Would I Lie To Myself?
Tips
Summary Of Element Two

Element Three
Getting To Know The Real You
Getting To Know Yourself
Where Are Your Dreams?
Are You A Satisfied Person?
Summary Of Element Three

Overview

In this part...

We all think we know who we really are. If someone asks us to describe ourselves, we can give them a whole list of qualities, thoughts and feelings, etc. that we think pretty much covers who we are. The problem is that most of our lists only really scratch the surface of our true character and abilities. They cover only those things about ourselves that we are prepared to look at. Unfortunately, that usually leaves huge parts of ourselves that we are ignorant about, and if you are ignorant about an aspect of yourself, then you cannot use it effectively toward your goals.

What we need to do is ask ourselves questions that we would not normally know to ask, and in this way we can open new doors to find the person we truly are. It is interesting how many times we are asked a question we have never been asked before and we find ourselves surprised by our answer. We find ourselves saying, "That's an interesting question, I've never really thought about that before, and I had no idea I felt that way."

Answering questions that we don't normally consider or think to ask ourselves can teach us so much about who we really are. This is crucial to finding your concept of success because the Real You is the foundation on which you will build that success.

Introduction

This *Successology* guide, surprisingly, is about you.

I stress that I do mean you; and who knows you better than you do? (That is rhetorical before you begin to answer.)

I would also like to make it clear that the parts and elements of this book will affect you differently than anyone else who reads it. The changes, advice, and benefits you gain will be different than those gained by your spouse, siblings, colleagues or friends (all of whom should definitely be encouraged to buy a copy of this book, by the way!).

Imagine your character as being an attractive pair of sunglasses. Each person's is a little different, with a different hue of glass coloring their surroundings in an original way, a way that is shared by no one else. The 'You' part of *Successology* needs those super-specs, so put them on now because this whole book only works if you apply it to your own personal situation!

Remember: This (along with life's other beneficial changes) is not a shake-and-bake solution (sorry). It requires effort (sorry again) and thought on your part (no apologies there).

You are Not Unique

Isn't it nice to know that there is no one quite like you?

You are very much unique. Genetically, you are an original. Amongst billions, you stand out in the crowd. Nice fuzzy feeling? But what if I told you that you are not really unique at all? What if I broke the news to you that there is more than one of you in this world, more than two of you, that in reality, there are three of you?

"What? This guy Scott is mad!!!" – I hear you scream.

Well, step away from your comfy "I am unique therefore I am special" zone, and let's explore this together. The concept of the Three You's is central to this book and to the **Xology Guides**. My philosophy on this matter is very different to other guides. Your consideration, understanding, and application of this theory in your life will dramatically change how far you will succeed and how you apply and read other self-help guides (see, I even help you benefit from other people's books).

When it was first suggested that the world was round and not flat, people cried, "Heretic!" and burnt the offenders at the stake!!! Bearing this in mind, and in case you start building the bonfire ready for my execution, I have taken the precaution of wearing flame-retardant underwear whilst you ponder this new concept; the idea that there are three of you walking this earth.

Prepare for all eventualities. Ponder all case scenarios, and plan action for each one. Never be caught off guard.

We are going to explore the Three You's Theory over the next few elements after you have had time to digest and mull over this new idea. New ideas are hard to accept. After all, we become secure and feel safe with what we know. Change means effort, a new way of thinking, and sometimes a new way of being. The best way to start on this path to change is to explore, listen, and to think.

The ability to listen and understand new concepts and ideas is crucial in your development. Understanding something is very different than agreeing with it. I do not expect you to agree with everything we discuss in these pages. But, if I can get you to ponder, think, and pontificate, then I have succeeded in starting you on the path to self-discovery and a path to success. Questioning is a huge part of discovery learning, and if I can perhaps get you to question things about yourself, then I feel I have accomplished something (always nice for facilitators and authors like me to feel).

"Who we are never changes. Who we think we are does."
Mary S. Almanac

So firstly, let us start with the concept that you need to learn more about yourself. Do you agree with that much? Good!

Over the next few pages, you will learn, develop, and expand your mind with the Three You's Theory, but to end the suspense, let me give you a synoptic overview of how you are not a single entity in this world.

 # Overview of the Three You's Theory

The Three You's Theory is comprised of:

The Real You - The inner you that lives inside your head.

The Projected You – The you that you would like the world to see.

The Perceived You – The you the world actually sees.

Sounds simple? Sounds stupid? It is neither! This is your new reality in a complex world, a world where an understanding of this makes you far more powerful, and one where you are more in control.

The secret to success is creating balance and harmony between the Three You's, (or "3Y's").

"In me I am me, out there who might I be, am I what you see?"
Lowi De Bell (1962 -)

Summary of Introduction

- You are the definition of success
- Real and lasting change is difficult
- Once started, success is a self-perpetuating energy (get a Newton's cradle and keep it somewhere conspicuous to remind you of this)
- You must be open to new ideas, not just in this guide but in life
- Success and growth present themselves in strange ways sometimes
- The Three You's Theory! The Real You, the Projected You and the Perceived You
- *Successology* examines all Three You's and introduces skills and ideas to develop them, and then puts them to work to facilitate your success

Element One

The Real You

The Real You is the person inside your head. The Real You is the person that only you know. It is the voice in your mind, it is the urges and the desires that seem too wild, silly or far-fetched to ever share with anyone.

The Real You is also the you that you might even be ashamed of. The Real You lives in a place where your inner child dwells, where your dreams and wishes are made. Many of us lock the doors to this place so tightly we forget it was ever there.

As a child you were naturally curious (remember all those eons ago?), you had an ability to create in a way that was unique to you, you had a vivid imagination, you had boundless energy and abilities and you believed you could do anything. As you grew, you were often discouraged away from your individuality so that you would conform and fit into the world. You believed in fantasy as a child, you believed you could achieve anything. Those beliefs, desires, hopes, dreams, and wishes are still there in the Real You, even if they are now hidden away.

Don't feel dismayed if you can't feel them. We will awaken them.

"Youth is not a time of life, it is a state of mind. You are as old as your doubt, your fear, your despair. The way to keep young is to keep your faith young. Keep your self-confidence young. Keep your hope young."
Luella F. Phean

Write down what your dreams were when you were a child. Where are those dreams now? How many were realized?

Your notes...

_____

_____

_____

_____

_____

_____

_____

_____

_____

_____

_____

As we strive to conform, to fit in, we lose sight of who we really are, what our purpose really is. Forgetting these things leads to a lack of fulfillment, sadness, depression, and a feeling of failure. But because we have forgotten, we do not know why we feel panicked, depressed, and stressed – we just know we feel this way.

www.ndnda.org - depression help site
—a website with depression help and advice

When you are alone (perhaps at night, driving in your car), you chat to yourself in your head. This is the Real You. You are constantly talking with yourself, even when having a real conversation with other people. We speak at approximately 200 words a minute and think at approximately 500 a minute. What happens to those excess 300 words a minute?   Imagine how much chat you really have with the Real You throughout the day. For the majority of the time, we hide these thoughts from everyone – after all, would you really share your very deepest thoughts with anyone?

The Kitchens of our Mind

Imagine for a moment that your life is a restaurant. Of course the windows are clean, the tables are neat, and the food is good (if we are careful). Perhaps some restaurants have handcrafted chandeliers, exotic menus, and fine silverware on the tables. Others may have plain but sturdy chairs with paper napkins, and a simple hearty buffet. Regardless of these differences, in the kitchens of all these restaurants, chaos is breaking lose, with trash on the floors, grease on the counters, smelly dish cloths, and sometimes much worse. The Real You is sometimes the messy parts of us that are kept from view, hidden behind heavy swing-doors, far from the more pleasant sitting areas of your image.

Tips

- **Keep a journal of your goals and wishes**
- **Use *Xology.com* to keep a private journal of your thoughts and activities (this is private, with your own user name and password)**
- **Make a list of things you don't like about yourself. Write a list of ideas of how you can change these things.**

My notes...
Don't like...   *Can change by...*

_____   _____
_____   _____
_____   _____
_____   _____
_____   _____
_____   _____
_____   _____

Summary of Element One

- You are far more boring now than when you were a child!
- Your childlike energy, vitality, and creativity are still somewhere inside you
- Think of all the things you keep in your "kitchen'"

Element Two

Who Knows You Best?

Some of us are lucky enough to let others into our "kitchens" or at least to look through the doors, and some of us are even luckier to have those people still love and care for us once they have peeked at our mess. In reality, I have yet to meet someone who is totally open about his or her inner self – one that has those swing-doors always open. It is almost impossible to do so. The purpose of this section of the book is not to encourage you to open wide your "kitchen doors" and suddenly declare your undying love to the local bank teller (to whom you have always been attracted), or to set off around the world suddenly on your life-long dream trek. I simply want you to start opening some of the locked doors in your head and accepting that it is normal to have those inner feelings. I want you to explore those dusty corridors and see what treasures are lying there after all these years. Maybe you'll be surprised.

I am not suggesting that some people who are close to you in your life do not know you at all; some of us are very fortunate to have very close companions, and such companions are often a part of our success.

These people include:

Spouses   Partners
Children   Colleagues
Parents   Friends

In *"Yahoo!"* poll, 23,000 people were asked "Who knows you best, aside from your partner?"

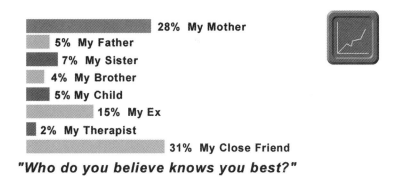

"*Who do you believe knows you best?*"

In **Part 3** (The Perceived You) you might be surprised to find that some of these people see your character, goals, and motivations very differently than you do.

Although you may have an openness with one or two close people, it is safe to say that the only person who really knows you *is* you. However, your current personal knowledge of yourself is probably limited to a small part of what your aspirations, preferences, strengths, and appealing idiosyncrasies really are.

But how can you get reacquainted with all these dusty parts?

Please do not misinterpret such questioning and topics with some Far Eastern philosophy – this really is all about you and your success.

Do you recognize that you might have lost touch with certain parts of the inner you, even with some of your core elements central to your existence? Your core contains your abilities, faith, personality, and other untapped traits. Your core contains the very elements that give you the potential to your success. These elements give you the drive and ability to strive, become recognized and have the faith to persevere. The first and most important thing to do is to be honest with yourself and find those elements within you. Even if you have been able to hang onto some core elements, much of the time you may have actually deceived yourself as to your true nature, or at least to some parts of it.

Why Would I Lie to Myself?

What makes us lie, especially to ourselves? One of the main reasons people lie is fear. Fear is a very powerful agent.

"If you do not tell the truth about yourself, you cannot tell it about other people."
Virginia Wolf (1882 – 1941)

www.radicalhonesty.com
- How being radically honest can transform your life

We are mainly afraid of:

Rejection – a powerful agent. But if we were to be rejected for something we believe in, then those rejecting us would not be worth knowing anyway. Don't fear rejection, and have faith in your beliefs.

Failure – a yucky feeling, but sometimes failures are important.

"Don't be discouraged by failure. Failure, in a sense, is the highway to success because every discovery of what is false leads us to seek after what is true. And every fresh experience points out an error which we shall, afterwards, carefully avoid."
John Keats (1795 - 1821)

I was teaching at a seminar in Las Vegas, and we were discussing failures. A member of the audience informed me that another lecturer had just told the last class to avoid failures at all costs. I was horrified. Failures teach us. As humans, we are fallible and prone to err. Experience can be gained from a failure. Don't be afraid of failure.

"The freedom to fail is vital if you are going to succeed."
Michael Korda

The Unknown – wait a minute!!! (shocked look on my face). Why be afraid of something unknown? If you don't know what it is, then how can you know what it is to be afraid of? Give me a huge hairy spider crawling up my leg, and I will be afraid. Give me something unknown, and I will be curious. You should try to imagine the unknown as a new experience, a situation of exciting and refreshing challenges.

"Apart from the known and unknown, what else is there?"
Harold Pinter (1930 -   )

Isolation – of course we do not like to feel alone. No man is an island. However, if you compromise your beliefs through fear of isolation, then you are already isolated in a crowd who thinks of you as something you are not. Find others who are like-minded to you—it is easy to do.

"Loneliness and the feeling of being unwanted is the most terrible poverty."
Mother Teresa (1920 - 1997)

There are many phobias, but few go as deep as those personal social fears that I have mentioned. However, do not underestimate the power of a phobia. If you have a phobia or fear of something that adversely affects your life, please do not ignore it. Rid yourself of it now so that we can move on together, uninhibited.

www.phobiaproducts.com
- Site for phobias and anxiety disorder products

We should recognize and analyze our fears so as to avoid the traps of lying to ourselves. Failure to do this might result in us simply being afraid of so much that we cease to really live.

Afraid
By
Scott

You're afraid to laugh
In case they think you are a fool

You're afraid to cry
In case they think you are weak

You're afraid to ask for help
In case they think you are stupid

You're afraid to risk
In case they think you are a loser

You're afraid to hope
In case they let you down

You're afraid to live
In case you die

You're afraid to be honest
In case they know all of these things about you

None of these fears are founded. Realize that all your thoughts are private and safe since no one (but you) can hear your thoughts (telepathy has yet to be a proven science, so worry not!). With nothing to be afraid of at this point, there is no reason to lie to yourself, and no harm (but bundles of good stuff) can come from an understanding of yourself.

So, with honesty in mind, I will ask you shortly to take a small test (I hate the word test as it indicates that you could fail with the wrong answers). There are no wrong answers, just honest answers. Remember, no one else will see or hear your thoughts.

This test examines who you really are and explores a few basic fundamentals necessary for both you and me to be sure of where you want to go and where you will in fact find success.

I encourage you to use a small notepad to make notes as you go through the book. Keep notes of points, targets, and answers to questionnaires. Make sure that this notebook can be kept safe so that you can feel at ease and be honest about yourself. Don't worry - I won't peek either.

 Tips

- **Write out a list of everyone that knows something private about you**
- **Write out your fears. Look for things that you wanted to do but didn't - why? Then cross through each fear in turn, and in its place write why that fear is unfounded**

Your notes...

Your notes continued...

_____

_____

_____

_____

_____

_____

_____

_____

_____

_____

_____

_____

_____

Summary of Element Two

- Realize that most human fears are unfounded. Furthermore, no harm will come from examining your faults and goals in the privacy of your thoughts

Element Three

Getting to Know the Real You

It is easy to assume someone else's identity, or rather, it is easy to assume someone else's values and goals (which is really very close to losing your own identity). Too often we adopt the attitudes, beliefs, and values of someone else simply because we admire them. This is wrong. As with a diamond, there are many facets to a personality and character; yours is unique to you. Staying true to your own character and strengths is what will make you an individual and potentially successful. Through life's turmoil and tests, only progress based on existing personal (not fabricated) strengths and desires will have any impact to succeed.

www.adcritic.com
- Watch the best commercials and see if they affect you!

It is very easy to start buying, traveling, deciding, retreating, and behaving differently because of outside influences. Television is one of those influences that is constantly in our lives.

98% of American households have a color TV!

Time Almanac

After a while, these superficial character devi-
ances (that are not really you) become habitual,
and we adopt those preferences and behaviors as
our own and then we wonder why we fail to stand
out, get noticed or even feel content.

"First we form habits, then they form us. Con-
quer your bad habits, or they'll eventually con-
quer you."
Dr. Rob Gilbert

Getting to Know Yourself

Ask yourself the following questions. Write
the answers out in as much detail as possible. Now would be a good time to start
using that notepad – your answers will be
useful for you to look back on:

If you could change one thing about your life, what would it
be?

What three principles would you fight for?

Which three people do you most admire and why?

What makes you most angry?

What makes you most happy?

How many times a day do you laugh?

Describe in single words how you feel emotionally about the
day ahead when you first wake up?

On the whole, how positive do you feel about your future and
also your current situation?

Getting to know yourself is paramount to finding success. If you don't know who you really are your life and career may continue to rub your feet as though you were hiking in someone else's boots.

 "Success is doing what you want to do, when you want, where you want, with whom you want, as much as you want."
Anthony Robbins

Run a bath, play some gentle music, dim the lights, and lay and think about your journey through life. Where did you change? Was it really for the best?

Where are Your Dreams?

 "A man is not old until regrets take the place of dreams."
John Barrymore (1882 - 1942)

As children, we are unashamed, unafraid of our dreams, and certain of our goals. As people grow, they lose the passion that fired those youthful dreams, they lose touch with who they are and what they feel.

www.greatnessbecomesyou.com
- Ways to set goals and how they should be made

To be more fulfilled in the adult world, people must first know what they want to achieve and how to be happy making that journey. Satisfaction should not be a destination but rather a means of transportation. I sometimes relate to the satisfaction and happiness of the goal simply by knowing I am moving towards it.

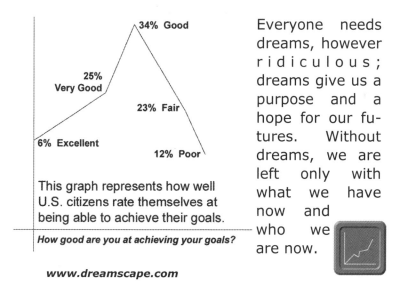

This graph represents how well U.S. citizens rate themselves at being able to achieve their goals.

How good are you at achieving your goals?

www.dreamscape.com

Everyone needs dreams, however ridiculous; dreams give us a purpose and a hope for our futures. Without dreams, we are left only with what we have now and who we are now.

Are You a Satisfied Person?

Answer the questions on the following pages by circling "YES" or "NO". Circle the "?" only if you are in genuine doubt. Take the questions slowly, consider each one carefully—this is not a timed challenge.

Do not be afraid to spend a few moments to discover your true feelings. Try to be as honest as possible. Answering truthfully will help you learn more about yourself.

Are you in the right profession? (If you could do any job in the whole wide world, would you choose the one are doing right now?)
YES   ?   NO

Would you describe yourself as having a positive outlook? (Do you believe in your life as it is, or are you just putting a brave face on it all?)
YES   ?   NO

Have you successfully overcome a challenge or crisis? (Have you really put it behind you, or do you still have bitterness, anger or resentment of it?)
YES   ?   NO

Do you look at your failures as an opportunity to learn? (Have you good feelings from your failures?)
YES   ?   NO

Do you feel emotionally secure?
YES   ?   NO

Can you accept criticism without feeling attacked? (All of the time?)
YES   ?   NO

Do you have close friends whom you can trust with a secret? (What about a big personal secret involving you?)
YES   ?   NO

Does the way you live match your personal values? For example: If you believe in honesty, are you truly honest?

YES   ?   NO

Do you create opportunities rather than wait for them?

YES   ?   NO

Do you feel that your present income covers your future costs?

YES   ?   NO

Do you have a hobby or interest that you do regularly? (And, do you do it well?)

YES   ?   NO

Do you feel that you are part of a mutually loving relationship?

YES   ?   NO

Do you have a sense of belonging?

YES   ?   NO

Is your income adequate?

YES   ?   NO

Do you get enough credit and praise for the things you do?

YES   ?   NO

Are you free from worry?

YES   ?   NO

When all possible has been tried, can you admit defeat?

YES   ?   NO

Do you have self-respect?

YES   ?   NO

Do you have a way of relaxing that invigorates you mentally and spiritually?

YES   ?   NO

Do you continually feel glad to be alive?

YES   ?   NO

Do you feel genuinely happy at least once every day?

YES   ?   NO

Do you keep yourself in shape without being fanatical?

YES   ?   NO

Are you willing to try something completely new? (Even something that is alien to you?)

YES   ?   NO

Do you want to continue learning as you progress in your life?

YES   ?   NO

Have you genuinely discarded some of your gender's stereotypes and prejudices?

YES   ?   NO

Do you make wishes often?

YES   ?   No

How many YES answers did you circle?

I circled _____ Yes's

Assessing your Answers

The closer to 26 "Yes" answers you circled, the nearer you are to being a completely satisfied person and the more likely it is that you are already being true to your own desires and goals.

Look at your "No" answers, and select one that you feel most strongly about. Write it out by using the format below.

Example:
I do not feel...*happy at least once a day.*

I could improve this by...*doing something I enjoy everyday. I enjoy...*

I can start this change by...*finding an activity that makes me happy and which is easy enough to fit into my day, such as ...*

When will I start to make this change?...*I will start tomorrow.*

Your notes...

_____

_____

_____

_____

_____

_____

_____

_____

_____

_____

Spend time looking at all your "No" answers, and apply the same approach given above. Your goal is to approach each of them in the same way so that you overcome every obstacle that prevents a "Yes" answer.

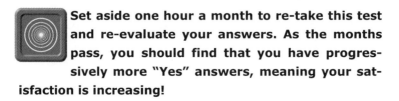 **Set aside one hour a month to re-take this test and re-evaluate your answers. As the months pass, you should find that you have progressively more "Yes" answers, meaning your satisfaction is increasing!**

Summary of Element Three

- Be careful that you are always true to yourself. It is easy to adapt / inherit the goals, preferences and principles of others
- Work on your Satisfied Questionnaire regularly to monitor your satisfaction
- Re-evaluate your general satisfaction with life using these questions on a regular basis

Element Four

The Enemies of Success

Being successful is very much a state of mind that leads to a state of being. As much as I can encourage you to reach inside yourself to develop and grow the elements within you which will transport you to a more successful way of being, it is important for you to be aware of some of the dangers and enemies you will meet along the way.

Many of these enemies are not physical foes that dwell in the dark alleys of the corporate world; they are dormant inside of you right now, ready to strike at any moment. These enemies can lead you away from self-fulfillment, from success itself to isolation, loneliness, and misery.

These enemies are often insipid and rather clever chaps who know just when to pounce on you when you are least expecting it. They are clever at disguising themselves and will often lead you astray without you even knowing that it is they who hold your hand.

You have to keep a constant vigil, a 24/7 watch for the attack of the enemies of success.

Knowing Your Enemies

Image is bad (it doesn't matter what you look like; it is what's inside that matters)

Rubbish, rubbish, rubbish! This type of attitude is the lazy person's approach to slovenliness! People will rarely give you the chance to show what is inside of you if you do not show them that you have put some effort into your presentation.

> *"The common practice of keeping up appearances with society is a mere selfish struggle of the vain with the vain."*
> **John Ruskin (1819 - 1900)**

You are a product, a self-contained package. Since ninety percent of a message is visual, you should do your darnedest to make sure you get the right message across. Get to that mirror immediately, and figure out how to make the best of what life has given you.

www.personalimagesinc.com
- Guide to portray a professional image for clients

Vanity is bad if you put the way you look above all else. But caring about what you look like is extremely important. It says, "This is me."

Revenge is Sweet

Not true! Revenge is a waste of energy. Whilst you are exacting revenge on someone, you are, in reality, showing that person that they mean enough for you to care about them in some way. The only difference between love and hate is a bridge called anger. Get over it!

"Surviving well is your finest revenge."
Morgan Nito

Turning the other cheek is not a form of pacifism and does not literally mean that you are some-one's punching-bag; simply put, it means you do not seek revenge.

When someone offends me and continues to hurt me regardless of the efforts I make with them, my greatest revenge is to erase them totally from my life. To me, they cease to exist. I refuse to give them any credence in my mind or my life.

www.revengeunlimited.com
- A fun site for getting light-hearted revenge on friends

Judging

Whilst you are pointing your finger at someone else, three of your own fingers are pointing back at you. It never ceases to amaze me how venomous and vitriolic people are as they pass sentence over others. Whilst you are wasting time looking so deeply at other people, you are not spending enough time analyzing yourself. It appears to me that some people seek to find mistakes and errors in others to keep attention from themselves; and also as a binky or a comfort blankie just to make themselves feel better. After all, "If Sally or Joe is *that* bad, maybe I am O.K. just the way I am. I would never..." Rubbish and hogwash (two of my favorite disparaging words). Get real with the program here! What is so important about Sally and Joe (or what they do) that should distract you from getting your life in order?

"We should be lenient in our judgment, because often the mistakes of others would have been ours had we had the opportunity to make them."
Dr. Alsaker

Jealousy

Jealousy is an evil little creature. We see someone with something that we want, and we become jealous. I know, I know, I know, I have heard all the excuses. "Susie didn't deserve to get that (I want it)", and "Jason didn't even work for it, it was handed to him on a silver platter (I want it)." Well, no matter how much you whine you are not going to get it. If someone has something that you like, get off your butt and go out and work for it (except get a bigger and better one). Whilst you sit crying about what Susie and Jason have, you are wasting valuable time in not getting it for yourself.

"Jealousy is the jaundice of the soul."
John Dryden (1631 - 1700)

Jealousy is also a form of recognition of your own failures. You need to realize that if you are showing or feeling jealousy towards someone or something, what you are really saying is that someone has something you want but can't have. You are recognizing that you are not capable of getting it for yourself, that you are inept, inadequate, useless, and floppy. So next time you feel those pangs of jealousy, slap it around the head and beat it away with a determination stick. Become determined that you will get the things you want, this is your life, and you are going to fill it with the things that make you happy.

www.queendom.com
- Test your susceptibility to jealousy

Warning: When I advise you to go out and get what you want, please take care not to become materialistic. It is easy to fall into the "I want" trap. "I want" can lead to a life spent trying to attain things to impress the Joneses. Remember: Things wear out, things age quickly, and towards the end of many people's journey, I find that most people find only true worth and value in the simple and meaningful things (they discard the previously valuable purchases as worthless). Thing-hunting can lead to debt, trouble, and strife; once you have obtained the "thing," another comes along that you need just as much. The list becomes endless. So, keep your want list under control and your horizons on an even keel.

Procrastination

"Never leave that till tomorrow which you can do today."
Benjamin Franklin (1706 - 1790)

This is the slippery slide down lazy man's alley. When you have plenty of things to do, procrastination comes along to detour you (hey, that rhymes!!!). The old adage "Why put off tomorrow what you can do today" is such a jewel to the successful person, so wear it with pride. I want you to get used to making lists, and lists, and lists. Make lists of all the things you can think of that need to be done in your life. Organize your lists into personal, private, and business. Then get cracking on demolishing them. You will feel so good, accomplished, and revitalized. Procrastination will be afraid to show its face around your life once you have done this.

www.selfsabotagebehavior.com
- Find out how much damage procrastination can do

Pride

Pride in its worst state is a one-way street to loneliness and isolation. I like to feel pride in my work, I like to feel proud of my daughter and I like to feel pride for the accomplishments of my friends. But this is not the type of pride I mean when we talk of a terrible trait. I refer to the sort of pride where you feel better than Sarah or Johnnie. This sort of pride is self-destructive. It is an easy trap to fall into when success begins to come your way. As success arrives, you feel better than others, you forget where you came from. To avoid this trap, remember your roots, remember who you are and remember that you are no better than anyone else – whoever they are. (If you do not agree with me, then you are not really absorbing what we chatted about in the judgment segment.)

Ignorance   *(lack of respect and manners)*

Ignorance is a terrible skill to possess. I call it a skill as it appears to me that many people go to great lengths to learn and perfect it. Ignorance is a neon sign to the rest of the world warning them to stay away from you. Ignorance comes in many shapes and forms; it generally results in an all-around lack of respect for your fellow man and a disdain to the pleasantries of etiquette. I am horrified how some people treat each other. In restaurants I sit in meetings, and in hotel lobbies I watch doormen, hosts, waiters and waitresses being treated as non-people. When people are ordering things, I hear the dreaded "Yes, I want ...", instead of "Please may I have...". In grocery stores, I watch people purchasing their goods without any pleasantries exchanged with the check-out staff. The world seems to be grinding down to a halt in the art of manners mainly due to ignorance. This becomes habitual. We expect our children to be polite but we show them that we ourselves are ignorant.

We should always use please and thank you whenever we interact with anyone we meet. You would be surprised at how many diners, for example, ignore the presence of another human being (the waiter/waitress) as their food is placed in front of them. It says a lot about you if you can stop your conversation for one moment to say, "Thank you." Truly successful people treat others with respect whatever their position and standing in society. Truly successful people have time for everyone.

Ignorance hates a smile, hates etiquette, and manners. Are you ignorant?

You Are What You Eat

"Tell me what you eat, and I will tell you what you are."
Anthelme Brillat-Savarin

I sometimes wonder if the conspiracy theory between the fast food restaurants and the weight loss companies is true. Could it be they are in cahoots? One industry encourages us to eat , save time, and have fun; the other industry then encourages us to lose the weight and repent. To save a few minutes in a day, we rush our food, order fast convenience foods or skip a meal altogether. I do hope the minutes you save on this in a day are well spent and worth it because they sure won't be there at the shortened end of your life.

In 2000 Americans spent more than $110 Billion on fast food...that's more than was spent on higher education!

Fast Food Nation

Unhealthy eating and indulgencies, although a common lure of the busy, ambitious or successful (and perhaps my worst failing), is a huge mistake. I know I need to work on this area of my life, do you?

Healthy Conscience
By Scott

*A double cheeseburger
With extra cheese
Some fries
Extra Large
Onion rings
An apple pie
A chocolate doughnut
With ice-cream side*

And a diet cola, please.

After you reach thirty years of age, your metabolism slows down one percent each year. So even those of you blessed with the "I never put on weight" fast metabolism cannot avoid the clogged arteries, high cholesterol, and blood pressure. Take my advice: Eat sensibly and let your body know you care. You would not put rubbish into your car's engine, so why put rubbish into your body's engine?

www.eatright.com
Healthy eating guides from American Dietetic Association

Science Magazine

 Tips

- **Keep a food and drink journal of everything you consume for just one week. You will be astounded at what you put into your body. From this journal you will be able to re-evaluate your diet**

Summary of Element Four

- You will be susceptible to the enemies of success.

    Complacency of Image: Always look your best

    Revenge: Avoid it even though you may have the authority or power to exact it

    Judging others: Stay focused on improving yourself, not criticizing others

    Jealousy: Avoid it by hard work and faith in yourself

    Procrastination: Use small cards to maintain to-do lists

    Pride: Never assume that you are better than anyone else. Do take pride in your strengths, and use them to help others

    Ignorance: Always treat everyone with respect, especially those who are normally ignored (i.e. servers / receptionists / hosts, etc.)

    Poor Health: Start to consider your eating and exercise habits. Treat your body right, and it will be there for the long haul

Element Five

Developing Yourself

When I was just starting out training employees and executives (many hundreds of years ago, it seems), I was once taken aback by the response of a 40-something corporate officer.

When I asked him to make one wish to acquire a brand new skill for himself without effort, he answered that he had learned everything he needed for life when he was in school and college. He continued to explain that he now refused to learn anything new! He was serious, and then he then proceeded to try and be as difficult as he could in the session. I worked hard with him, and ultimately he became motivated to learn many new things, perhaps some of which helped him to become the CEO he is today.

Until that time, I had assumed everyone understood that life is a continuing lesson (although the important bits seem to be hidden most of the time) that you have to seek out, learning on a daily basis to benefit and progress toward your goals.

"Learning how to learn is life's most important skill."
Tony Buzan

Life Lessons 101

Unlike our "fully educated friend," most people find that standard education doesn't come close to preparing them for either working or adult life.

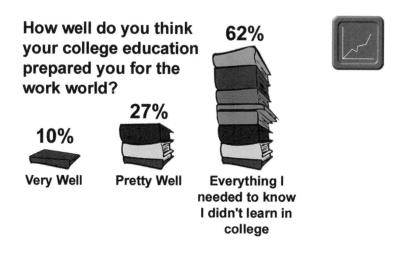

How well do you think your college education prepared you for the work world?

62%

27%

10%

Very Well

Pretty Well

Everything I needed to know I didn't learn in college

www.monster.com

Can't I Just Bluff It?

Bluffing is dangerous because it is based on nothing (aside from your ability to maintain a façade), and only nothing can ultimately result from it.

When we bluff, we run the risk of others seeing behind the curtain. Sometimes we don't realize that we are bluffing. It is only when we discover that where we have arrived at is not where we meant to go do we recognize that something is wrong, and we feel disillusioned.

**www.indignantonline.com/humor/
presentation.htm**
- Learn how to bluff your way through life - (but don't
really– this is JUST for fun)

The cause of so much stress, turmoil, and unhappiness is mainly due to people's own disillusionment. There is a growing and constant list of rich and famous people who either die young or are revealed to have suffered depression. Ever wonder why? Weren't they successful people? I am sure they appeared to many to be so, at least materially. However, as success in life is also about personal contentment and fulfillment, maybe some of those celebrities would now choose a different course (a different way of being) if they had it to do over again.

So in finding success for you, it is vital that you decide on a balance between all of life's elements - some of which are listed below:

Financial
Status
Community Recognition
Family Recognition
Lifestyle
Possessions
Family
Faith
Societal Impact

Write each of the items out, and rate each one on its true importance to you.
5 points = Vital   1 point = Unnecessary

Your notes...

_____

_____

_____

_____

_____

_____

_____

_____

_____

_____

_____

_____

_____

Some people have a tough time differentiating between their own desires and those they think they should have. Do you really want unfathomable wealth, or could you be happy simply with sufficient money to live comfortably? Constantly examine your own expectations and goals. Is a new and expensive car a real requirement or a marker and symbol of your success? Again, these elements also come into question when exploring the difference between the Three You's. Whatever your blend of success elements happens to be, all well and good, just make sure you are not chasing a goal that doesn't bring you what you really need. In other words, be careful what you wish for - you might just get it.

I see people on a regular basis who are driven to new heights to achieve what they *think* they see as success only to wake up feeling a strange unrest and wondering which accomplishment or purchase is missing. They will never know.

 Answer the following questions:

What materialistic possession could you NOT live without?

Whom could you NOT live without?

Which of the above is more important?

What does this tell you?

Your notes...

_____

_____

_____

_____

_____

_____

_____

 Tips

- **Take up a new hobby, and work over months at perfecting it**

- **Become more creative. Write poetry, draw sketches, and keep them as reference materials**
- **Write a list of what you like about yourself. Now work at developing these things**
- **Enroll in night school**
- **Put aside one special night a week to spend with your family and loved ones. Make it fun— a board game, cards, wholesome movies, etc.**

Your notes...

_____

_____

_____

_____

_____

Summary of Element Five

- You are still in school. Never stop learning. Write in your notepad one new fact or lesson that you learn each day
- The effort it takes to bluff an interest or skill could be well applied to generating a genuine one
- Take a lesson from the rich and famous; never assume that money and status equals happiness
- The first step in achieving success is defining what it is for you. Make a list of all the things that do and/or would make you happy. This will be your blueprint

Element Six

You Are What You Surround Yourself With

As your success stems from your own traits, you may want to develop more personal strengths. It may be easier than you think, as many of us have oodles of abilities lying dormant just beneath the surface waiting for the chance to grow and prosper.

A great way to develop new strengths is by exposing yourself to positive influences and pastimes. What you surround yourself with is your choice; no one can force you to do what you don't want to do or be where you don't want to be. You can create some good results by adding (or curbing) some elements to your lifestyle - all within your control.

Moderation in all things is really the key. As you read the following section, remember that too much of anything is not a good thing. You have only one life with a single, limited resource – Time. How you spend your quota of this valuable resource, or what you do with it in one area means that you cannot spend it on another. The world is watching, so take warning – you are what you surround yourself with.

Elements that Affect Your Character

Reading

Reading is a wonderful thing, yet it is remarkable how few books people read. With fiction and non-fiction titles filling up the ever-increasing number of bookstores, you should try and spend time at least once a week perusing the shelves to find something of interest to you. Magazines, websites, and newspapers: There is a plethora of material to titillate and tantalize your mind, awaken your imagination, and expand your knowledge.

"The greatest gift is the passion for reading. It is cheap, it consoles, it distracts, it excites and it gives you knowledge of the world and experience of a wide kind. It is a moral illumination."
Elizabeth Hardwick (1916 -   )

Reading increases your command of the English language, it increases your ability to communicate, and it gives you a broader historical and situational knowledge base. Reading can relax the mind before going to sleep, aiding in a good night's rest. However, if you spend your time reading too much, you could lose out on relationships, friendships, and life (remember: all things in moderation).

Make a list of all the great books you have read. Now make a list of all the great titles you know that you haven't read. Now, go read them.

Your notes...

_____

_____

_____

_____

_____

People

People are what make the world go around.

www.wsu.edu:8080~dee/world.htm
- Learn about cultures around the world

The wonderful thing about life is the diversity of cultures and the variety of people. Travel enhances our ability to expand our understanding of the world in which we live. Much as I encourage you not to judge, you should be aware of those you choose for close friends. If you hang around with slimy people, don't be surprised if you become slippery yourself. On the other hand, if you only socialize with one type of person and have only one circle of friends, you could be missing out on so much diversity in life. Learning about people is so edifying and also enhances your people skills.

"People who need people are the luckiest people in the world."
Bob Merrill (1890 – 1977)

Music

I find music one of the most stimulating things; my taste is incredibly varied. Right now as I write these words to you, I am listening to *Joaquin Rodrigo Guitar Concerto*. Find a range of music (instrumental, if possible) that relaxes, motivates, and invigorates you. Explore and enjoy this challenge. See how diverse you can be.

"Just as certain selections of music will nourish your physical body and your emotional layer, so other musical works will bring greater health to your mind."
Hal A. Lingerman

It is said that music can conjure up and bring back vivid memories. Classical music is wonderful for the creative mind and gives a fabulous ambience to any room. However, rock, pop, jazz, and rap, etc., are equally great, depending on your mood. Fill your life with music, and you will feel the benefits. Music is a powerful stimulant; however, if you devote too much of your time listening to music with violent lyrics and messages, you could become desensitized to the kindness of the world, including your own.

www.musiccity.com
- Latest news on music and artists

Pornography

There is a fine difference between art and pornography. Pornography is often frowned upon. I am not here to lecture you about the rights and wrongs of pornography and its effect on society, but as with all things, you should be aware of anything that can have an addictive quality.

"Its avowed purpose is to excite sexual desire, which, I should have thought, is unnecessary in the case of the young, inconvenient in the case of the middle-aged and unseemly in the old."
Malcolm Muggeridge (1903 -   )

If you look at pornographic images you could become less sensitive to morality and also suffer from depleted respect for your fellow man.

Pubs/Bars

Sometimes going to the bar with your friends is a great way to spend an evening; fun and laughter can be had. Socializing is a wonderful tool for bonding and freeing yourself of stress.

However, please remember that alcohol (even in the smallest of quantities) has an effect on our judgment and reasoning. Take care how much you drink if you do not want a red face in the morning. Most importantly, I advocate never drink and drive. This rule shows great respect for yourself and for the community in which you live. It also shows restraint.

"He that goes to bed thirsty (not drunk), rises healthy."
George Herbert (1593 – 1633)

Respect and restraint are qualities the successful person possesses. It is also unprofessional to drink more than a single drink when with business associates of any kind, especially at staff parties.

Time

Respect of time is crucial for the successful person. I have met so many business people who are always running late. When people run late, they are showing poor judgment in time management and a lack of respect for the person who is on time. Everyone occasionally has unforeseen challenges that throw their schedule haywire, but this should be the exception and not the rule.

Successful people have high regard for time (their own as well as other people's). Bad time management shows inefficiency and gives the appearance of disorganization and laziness (something you should avoid). Good time management reduces stress and indicates an efficient individual.

"Time equals Life. Therefore, waste your time and waste of your life, or master your time and master your life."
Alan Lakein

Stress

This is an increasingly common factor in life. Although a completely stress-free life could never be a reality, we can avoid and diminish the factors that cause stress. Successful people have control and therefore they can control the situations that lead to stress. Stressful situations lead to a stressful self. Stress can be reduced and even removed at times through good management procedures, by organization, planning (using to-do list cards), and effective time management.

"Pain of the mind is worse than pain of the body."
Publilius Syrus (1st Century B.C.)

Physical Being

You only have one body, so look after it. Successful people start by respecting the most important thing in their lives – their own bodies. Imagine the message you send out when you show little or no respect to your own being. How can a company give you responsibility over their finances or staff when you show that you have no responsibility to yourself? Exercise leads to higher endorphin levels, which leads to happiness and energy. Less exercise leads to feelings of tiredness and apathy. Look after your tool of the trade (your body and mind); I know contractors who spend more time keeping their ratchet set in order than they do working on reducing their beer-bellies!

"To avoid sickness, eat less, to prolong life, worry less."
Chu Hui Weng

Environment

You can choose where you live. If you live in a city, expect more stress (through increased traffic and people) but greater diversity. If you live in the country, expect less stress but less diversity. Your home is your castle; therefore, you should make it a place not just to eat and sleep but a special place to live. Your home

The National Urban Institute

should reflect you as a person. The décor, the pictures, the ornaments, and the ambience should all say something about you. Your home should have a quiet area, a room or place where you can relax in peace and quiet. Your home should be organized and well maintained. A pride in your environment reflects a pride in yourself. You should be able to invite people back to your home at any time without fear that it is a mess. A successful person does not just have a clean, tidy, and pleasant home when expecting guests; it should be this way all the time. Success is not a part-time thing, it is a way of life.

"You are a product of your environment. So choose the environment that will best develop you toward your objective. Analyze your life in terms of its environment. Are the things around you helping you toward success -- or are they holding you back?"
W. Clement Stone

Conscience

Your conscience is a wonderful tool; it is your truth-sayer that gives you an insight beyond the messages from the verbal, explicit world. Your conscience will lead and direct you to make the right decisions. When you get that gut feeling, listen to it. Successful people are in tune with their conscience, they have morality in all their dealings and use their conscience to ensure what they are doing falls within the boundaries of what they know is right. If you ignore your personal advisor, you will make more mistakes and feel guilty. A guilty conscience leads to stress (remember, something we want to avoid). A clear conscience not only avoids stress, it makes you feel happy with yourself, as well.

"Those who follow their conscience directly are of my religion; and, for my part, I am of the same religion as all those who are brave and true."
Henri IV (1533 – 1610)

Knowledge

It is said that knowledge is power. Never have truer words been spoken. But as we know, ultimate power leads to ultimate corruption. That is a little bit of an oxymoron. However, since we can never have ultimate knowledge, I do not think we need to worry (phew!).

Knowledge can be gleaned from many sources: TV, radio, books, the Internet, and probably most importantly, from people. As I travel giving keynotes, seminars, and workshops, I always feel honored that I can share my information with so many people. But I am always aware that there is no one in my audience who cannot also teach me. Everyone I come in contact with has something to share with me. And I listen. Successful people listen and learn from all those around them.

"Knowledge is the mother of all virtue; all vices proceed from ignorance."
Proverb

Listening

The world is a most stimulating place and the people in it even more stimulating. Let them stimulate you. Increasing your knowledge leads to a greater understanding of the world. You can never know too much, but apply and expose your knowledge carefully. No one likes a smart ass! So listen more than you speak.

*"Knowledge is gained by learning; trust by
doubt; skill by practice; love by love."*
Thomas Szasz (1920 -   )

Faith

Without some faith in something, I think life is
simply not worth living. Everyone needs faith in
something. Successful people put their faith in
themselves, their beliefs, their company, and their
loved ones.

*" Faith consists in believing when it is beyond
the power of reason to believe. It is not
enough that a thing is possible for it to be believed."*
Voltaire (1694 – 1778)

With faith comes optimism, with faith there is
hope. A lack of hope leads to a pessimistic life. I
am not preaching religion to you; by faith I mean
a faith in an idea, person, object or a higher being, etc. In other words - Hope.

Etiquette

I cannot overstate the importance of manners to

you. Success demands manners and etiquette. You can make the biggest impression with the smallest words. Knowing how to act appropriately is the essence of the successful person in the business world. By understanding etiquette, you can avoid embarrassment for yourself as well as those around you. Many feel that etiquette and manners give an air of class and snobbery. I say to them that I treat others as I wish to be treated. Where is the snobbery in that? I also refuse to accept the concept of class which is why I treat everyone with the same amount of respect and manners.

"Etiquette means behaving yourself a little better than is absolutely essential."
Will Cuppy (1884 - 1949)

Appearance

Your appearance says more about you than you could imagine. Ninety percent of a message is in its visuality. Do not be ashamed to take pride in the way you look. When you walk into a room,  you have already made a statement of who you are and what you stand for.

"Your appearance, he said to me, is the gauge by which you will be measured; try to manage that you go beyond yourself in after times, but beware of ever doing less."
Jean Jacques Rousseau (1712—1778)

Respect

The successful person always treats others as he or she would like to be treated. Enough said.

Attitude

Attitude is everything to the successful person. It is to the inward person what image is to the outward. In other words, your attitude says as much about you as the clothes you wear.

"Our attitudes control our lives. Attitudes are a secret power working twenty-four hours a day, for good or bad. It is of paramount importance that we know how to harness and control this great force."
Tom Blandi

At the risk of repeating myself, I will! Moderation in all things. Time is your most valuable commodity; **do not** waste it! (Am I being tough enough on you here?)

 Tips

- **List all the positive things that you feel add to your life—work on expanding them**
- **List all the negative things that are part of your life—get rid of them**
- **Re-read this element, and list under the same headings any of the things you do which fall into that category, i.e., reading—what you read and how much time you spend reading**

Your notes...

_____

_____

_____

_____

_____

_____

_____

_____

_____

_____

_____

_____

Summary of Element Six

- What you choose to watch on your television, play on your stereo, or look at has an effect
- Surround your life with the positive inputs, including literature, people, music, good health, and a supportive home atmosphere that recharges your batteries and acts as a safe haven from the world
- Evaluate what is in your life and consider amending, deleting or adding to it

Element Seven

And finally...

Time is your greatest ally and yet your worst en-
emy. Liken your journey in life to a dance. When
you are first born, the music seems fast and
never-ending; as you age, the music slows and
slows until finally the last beat is played.   With
this in mind, I end this part with a poem entitled
The Dance of Life. I feel it appropriate, and I hope
you will indulge me by reading it to yourself. If
you would like to see the colored, animated version with music, please feel free to visit :

www.1stCo.com

The Dance of Life
By
Scott

For the very young the dance has just begun
With the rhythm fast
Not knowing they won't last
The beat goes on
They think they know the song
The words of this tune
Will be forgotten too soon

Now a child they call, to go to the ball
It's only fair
They dance with care
Each movement stepped
They think they are adept
Their heart runs fast
Their role seems cast

Now a teenage rave, to their dance a slave
It's now a passion
To stay with the fashion
Some begin to falter
The learned steps alter
To a beat slightly slower
As their heart rates lower

Then a different key, a new melody
Into married hymns
Come flailing limbs
And a harmony begins
As a new baby sings
The chorus seems wrong
They don't recall this new song

But the beat suddenly halts,
and turns into a waltz
Not liking it before
They prefer 1, 2, 3, more
Now they can hear from the beginning
The beat of their own heart singing
Although its thud sounds so grim
Counting the Dance of Life in

The Adage is now here
and syncs with their own fear
They realize in fright
That their dance wasn't right
They want to restart the refrain
They want to dance it again
But the Last Dance is for all
Death closes this Ball

Summary of Element Seven

- Don't waste your Dance of Life!!!

Part One Conclusion

To be truly successful and have a good shot at getting what we want, we need to know ourselves - truly know ourselves. Only in this way can we see what it is that we need in our lives to achieve our own personal and, more importantly, meaningful success.

If you do not strive to find the Real You, then you will be forever living someone else's life and chasing their dreams. True, satisfying success cannot be found by living that kind of life.

If you strive to find the Real You and build a strong foundation (think of it like a well-researched business plan for your life), then you have given yourself the necessary platform and tools to achieve what your heart TRULY desires.

Part Two

The Projected You

Overview
> In This Part

Introduction

Element One
> Image
> How Will This Help Me Be More Successful?
> Image Assessment
> Tips
> Your Inward Image
> Tips
> A Warning!
> Summary Of Element One

Element Two - Verbal Communication
> We Are Like Cars
> Speech
> Tips
> Language In The Workplace
> Tips
> Summary Of Element Two

Element Three - Non-Verbal Communications
Introduction
What Is Body Language
How Body Language Is Read
Improving Your Body Language
Tips
Summary Of Element Three

Element Four - Written Communications
Your Image Emissary—Correspondence
Electronic Mail
Tips
Summary Of Element Four

Element Five - Listening Skills
Listening or Hearing?
Tips
Summary of Element Five

Element Six - Etiquette
Introduction
How Does Etiquette Affect Us?
Simple Effective Etiquette
Professional Etiquette
Summary of Element Six

Element Seven
Your Projected Life Through The Hourglass
So?
Using Time
Time Management
Multitasking
Take A Break?
How To Use A Break
Why Should A Break Be Taken
Tips
Summary of Element Seven

Element Eight - Health

Strength To Persevere
Tips
Summary Of Element Eight

Element Nine - Assertiveness

Strength Of Character
How To Be More Assertive
Achievements
What Would Make Most People Happy
Summary Of Element Eight

Part Two Conclusion

Overview

In this part...

Some of us feel that as long as we have a nice house, a fancy car, great clothes, etc., then people will see us as happy and successful. This says to me that the appearance of success to these people is actually more important than actual success. For me, I'll take the real happiness and success, thank you very much. On the other hand, others see the Projected You as totally superficial. They might say, "It only matters what a person is like on the inside" and try to avoid giving their image much consideration.

If you ask me (and I'm assuming you are), both of these views will hinder your path to success.

We must accept that we live in a world where most of the people we know don't actually know us at all. This begs the question, "So, who do they know?" if not the Real You. Well it makes sense to me to believe that it must be the impression of you or Projected You.

Remember, too, that this is a world of stereotypes and shortcuts—that really taking the time to get to know your noble qualities is too much time to take, and in a business setting, maybe it is.

We need to know what people are judging us on, which of your facets are most apparent (for these few shards of your character will be the basis of the "complete you" in their eyes) and which existing elements we can adapt to give the right message about who we are.

Introduction

And now we move on to the second you, the Projected You. This is the you that you want the
world to see. This is the you that you hope will impress and make people want to sit up and listen.
The Projected You is a difficult person to maintain.
If you try and please others too much, you run the
risk of losing sight of the Real You, and you live an
existence based solely on what everyone else expects of you. If you concentrate solely on being
the Real You, you run the risk of being considered
too eccentric and off the wall for most, and you
will live an existence based on a self-centered you
in a selfish world. It sounds an impossible mix to
get right, doesn't it? Well, it is not impossible. But
it is challenging, and your rewards could be great.
Isn't that why you are reading this book?

The real secret to success is to ensure that the
Projected You is based strongly upon the Real
You.

If the Projected You is accepted by the
world and rises through the steps to success, you want to know that it is achieving
the things that the Real You wants
(without this, a lack of fulfillment will ensue).
Some of the most successful people in the world -
from pop stars and movie stars to political figure
heads - have shown great signs of depression and
stress, some even turning to drugs or committing
suicide through unhappiness. Perhaps they really

did feel a lack of fulfillment. How is it possible that people who have seemingly found success, fame, and fortune are still unhappy? It is obvious that fame and fortune are not the key to real success, happiness, and fulfillment. Fame and fortune are what the world tells us success is. This I do not believe. If, for example, fortune is success, then Bill Gates must have achieved it and would not continue to work (after all, he is one of the richest men this world has ever seen). No, there is more to it all than money.

Success is all about balancing the Real You against the Projected You with the Perceived You – and NEVER losing sight of who you really are inside. Later in this book, in **Part 4** (please don't cheat and go looking for it), I will explain all the scientific equations and formulas for you to test out and play with. The *Xology* website will also assist you.

www.Xology.com
- Further Successology resources and tests

So after you feel you know what this is all about, go and check it out and discover even more about you and your life.

In this part of *Successology,* we will look at how to put the inward you (the Real You) into a format that will be successfully coupled with the Projected You. We will also discuss the facets of success as applied to the Projected You.

You may be familiar with some of the subjects covered on the following pages, but do not under-estimate the importance of what is being discussed. Too often we feel because we have heard something, or because we think we are familiar with a principle, we must be experts in that subject and proficient at it. This is a fallacy. If you can apply the following topics to your life, you will be on your way to a successful future. But remember, it is not simply a matter of doing these things, it is a matter of being !!!

This part of *Successology* exposes all of the necessary skills and considerations needed to successfully project the Real You to the world.

"Success is a journey, not a destination."

Ben Sweetland

Element One

Image

Looking your best should be everyone's desire (although I have a harder task than most—I have been told I have an excellent face for radio), and with this in mind, many new image ideas have been tested, amended, and reapplied. As is so often the case, by the time a chosen "look" is just right, fashions change and most people are once again left in the dark. The subject of image and personal presentation is designed to keep successful professionals informed in a changing business world. Following the rules of personal presentation will bridge the gap between looking good and looking great.

"All the World's a stage, and all the men and women merely players…"
As You Like It – William Shakespeare (1564-1616)

Performers involved in any live show are given a 30-minute call during which they prepare for their performance. Even the most experienced performers receive such a call. This time is used to warm up both vocally and physically, put on make-up, dress, rehearse lines, practice movement, etc. Such a routine has become mandatory to ensure both the performer's and the show's success.

When you leave home in the morning, the day's performance begins.   Looking and sounding fantastic ensures a successful "show." To make your show the best possible, you should also have a 30-minute call so that you can get organized. Find a routine to best suit your individual needs.   This regime should be established carefully and implemented religiously.

www.businessclothingdirectory.com
- An up-to-date directory of the most recent business fashions.

How Will This Help Me Be More Successful?

Business communication is dependent upon its visual element. Managers, peers, clients, customers, and staff should all enjoy a high level of professionalism through presentation. To be a success within a professional environment, it is important to have the attention of colleagues and associates; to do this, a professional look is essential.

"Your image is your window dressing to your store."
Lowi De Bell (1962 -)

Paying close attention to personal presentation demonstrates a strong sense of self-worth. Qualities such as value, care, and consideration are very important to customers and associates. Demonstrating these traits will help you gain respect from your fellow professionals and help instill confidence within you.

Image Assessment

Evaluate yourself on the following aspects of your personal presentation. Circle a number to denote your ability in each area. Don't worry, and try to be honest and objective.

 Circle each of the following elements as follows:

0-Poor   1—Below Ave   2—Ave   3-Above Ave   4- Excellent

General Manners
           0   *1*   *2*   *3*   *4*
Dining Etiquette
           0   *1*   *2*   *3*   *4*
Fashion Sense
           0   *1*   *2*   *3*   *4*
Grooming (Hair, Skin)
           0   *1*   *2*   *3*   *4*
Communication Skills
           0   *1*   *2*   *3*   *4*
Voice
           0   *1*   *2*   *3*   *4*
Social Ability (Parties, etc)
           0   *1*   *2*   *3*   *4*
Confidence
           0   *1*   *2*   *3*   *4*
Gesticulations
           0   *1*   *2*   *3*   *4*
Presentation Skills
           0   *1*   *2*   *3*   *4*

Physical Fitness

0	1	2	3	4

Eye Contact

0	1	2	3	4

Add up your score to see how your image is looking.

Image Assessment Results

0—11   Oh, Dear
Your image is doing you an injustice. Spend time on considering how your image could be improved. Many small changes make a big difference.

12—24   Average Image
Those who score in this level have an average, unobtrusive image. No real attention is given and nothing special happens as a result.

25 – 32   Above Average Image
To score in this section shows that you do make the effort but are not crystal clear about what is best for you. You are conscious of your image and have the will to improve rapidly. With a little honing, your image can do wonders for you.

33 – 40   Superior Image
You have a firm grasp on how to maintain an excellent image. Maybe you have invested a great deal of time considering how to perfect your business image, and it has paid off. With an image like yours, success will always be within reach - Well done!

First impressions are vitally important and essential to ensure that your image is at its finest at all times. By following some very simple guidelines, you can make the most of the tools readily available and portray a positive impression before speaking a single word!

"Mistrust first impulses; they are nearly always good."
Talleyrand (1754 – 1838)

 Tips

- **Get a new hairstyle - a change can be positive, and it will also help to accent other personality and character changes**
- **Examine your wardrobe, and replace older items—try to create an even and matching style for the entire week. Visit the mall and try a few different styles, colors, and designs**
- **Go bargain hunting for clothes during department store sales**
- **Look at what your colleagues are wearing for ideas**
- **Pens and gadgets are a great way to enhance your image**
- **Your work area reflects your image. Spruce it up. Include a plant and a photo or two**
- **Clean out your car, make it smell nice and get it washed regularly**
- **Change your deodorant / aftershave / cologne / perfume—it is amazing how scent changes your mood**
- **Ladies: Try new make-up colors**
- **Go swimming, exercise—not only will this help your health but you will look and feel invigorated**
- **Men: Wear tie pins (no novelty ones) for a little panache!**

Your Inward Image

When we wake up in the mornings, sometimes we look in the mirror and groan (I do most mornings). It is at that moment we see in all its glory our true physical self: un-kempt, tired, messy-haired, sleepy eyed, wrinkles, saggy, unshaven and unmade faces.

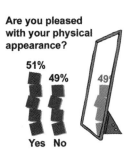

Are you pleased with your physical appearance?

51%
49%
49
Yes No

www.dreamscape.com

We transform ourselves into something more pro-fessional and then boldly strut out to face the world.

Through the day, we spend much of our time looking at others and their actions with the same critical eye with which we first viewed ourselves in the mirror that morning.

People need to carry a personal "personality mir-ror" with them at all times. Imagine if we spent as much time on improving ourselves as we do on critiquing others. Imagine if we put as much en-ergy into being better people as we do in feeling superior to those around us.

Perhaps we look critically at others so as to divert attention from looking at our own naked person-alities. After all, whilst we are giving our attention to others and how bad they are, we don't have time to look at ourselves to see how bad we really are.

However, the old adage comes to mind again: When you point a finger at someone else, three of your own fingers point right back at you.

The image you portray to the world is not just a physical one. You can make the packaging as fanciful and exuberant as you like but once someone opens the box, the packaging is forgotten. What is inside the box becomes the only thing that counts.

 Tips

- **Do something good every day**
- **Smile at people**
- **Drive your car with consideration for other motorists**
- **Listen to some classical music on your way to work—it will inspire you**
- **Work on saying Please and Thank You to people**
- **Read a good book, just a few pages a day**
- **Join a service group, and help your community**
- **Try to find something nice to say to your co-workers every day**

 Add Your Own Tips
Use your notepad to add to this and other Tips Lists. Also let me know what tips you find useful for each element. Email me directly at: ***Scott@1stco.com***

Your notes...

Your notes continued...

_____

_____

_____

_____

_____

_____

_____

_____

_____

A Warning

I always like to argue as the devil's advocate, and with this in mind, I would like to contradict what I have written (although I truly believe it). I have met many, many people through my travels, and I have been fortunate to have met some wonderful people. However, some of the people I have met fall into a category I like to call the "Sow's Ear." These are the people who dress and look success-ful but something is amiss. These are the people I liken to the fabulously wrapped gift that you tear open to discover it is something that you do not even want.

There is a wonderful Aesop Fable that ex-emplifies this point (I have rewritten it). It goes something like this:

The Ass & The Lion's Skin

"Once upon a time there was an Ass. His mother was a horse and his father was a donkey. He wasn't a very clever Ass (as was common among his type) and he was laughed at by all the other animals that lived in the forest for being so slow, easy to dupe and so prone to accidents.

On one particular day as the Ass was wandering aimlessly, admiring the flowers, and the other simple pastimes that an Ass enjoys - he came across a lion's skin lying on the floor. Finding play in everything, the Ass was content to toss the skin into the air until by accident the lion skin flopped and fell over his back - with paws hanging down covering his legs and the head covering his nose.

As the Ass started to try to shake off the lion's skin, a little rabbit happily hopped through the forest (this rabbit, by the way, had laughed particularly harshly at the Ass that very morning for walking into a tree!). The rabbit stopped, the smile left his face, and he shrieked seeing a huge lion. The rabbit ran away terrified. Well, the Ass was most impressed by the rabbit's reaction, and he finally concluded after many hours of deliberation (he took a long time to figure things out) that the rabbit actually thought he was a lion.

The Ass then spent the afternoon jumping out at the birds, the squirrels, and other rabbits. When the Ass managed to scare even the fox, he was so pleased and excited that he let back his head and let out a huge "Brraaaayyyy" (for that's how asses laugh).

Suddenly, the fox stopped his retreat, the birds stopped flying, and even the rabbits stopped running away. All the animals turned back. The fox walked up to the Ass and said, "When I first saw you, I was afraid because you looked like a lion, you jumped out at us like a lion and I thought you were a lion. But as soon as you opened your mouth, I knew you were an ass!"

Beware of becoming an ass in lion's clothing. As Aesop himself said:

"Fine clothes may disguise, but silly words will disclose a fool."

What does this teach us? It teaches us that we are bound to fall down if our image is *so* false as to completely disguise our true nature. (Stay true to who and what you are.) Just because you dress like a lion does not mean you are a lion. There is much more to being successful than dressing so. Find images that compliment you and not those images that misrepresent you. This is not to say that you cannot greatly improve your dress and grooming—simply make sure that you are comfortable with the end result.

"A strong, positive self-image is the best possible preparation for success."
Joyce Brothers (1928 -   )

Summary of Element One

- It is important to convey the Real You through the Projected You
- Use a 30-minute call each morning as you dress to get ready for your performance
- Are you dressed equally to the best-dressed person in your office / department? You should be
- Use personal presentation to reflect the Real You. If a briefcase is out of character for you, don't get one. If a formal suit isn't you, don't wear one - find a suitable compromise
- Keep your image yours—it will make you comfortable and keep the Projected You real and genuine to inspection
- Don't be an ass in lion's clothing—none of the lions or the other forest animals will appreciate it!

Element Two

Verbal Communication

We Are Like Cars

I don't know anything about cars (or computers) but I do know that just like cars, our bodies are tools that need maintaining.

Both of the cars below will perform their function by moving from point A to point B. The difference between them is how they accomplish this task. One car has been maintained and pampered; it has been restored, polished, and looks good. Communication skills, especially verbal skills, need just as much maintenance, time and care to provide a good image.

Both cars will get from A to B...

...which one would *you* drive?

Proper driving skills must be learned and practiced. All too often, people neglect to consider what tools and skills are needed in their professional and personal lives. Some people are aware of such skills but have never learned how to use them correctly. Maybe it's time for a little drivers' ed on communicating.

 "Don't just learn the tricks of the trade. Learn the trade."
James Bennis

After driving for many years, it is easy to form bad habits. This is also true regarding communication. For example: People drive too fast - people forget that pace and pro-nunciation are important. People fail to plan and time their journeys to be efficient and direct - people do not think about what they want to say, so they end up setting out in the wrong direction, causing descriptions and explanations to be lengthy and confusing. After using language for many years (many, many years, in my case) we can get lax in our usage. People often use slang and abbreviations to shorten speech.

It is important to recognize the benefits that can be reaped from additional effort in personal communications. So let's leave any verbal faux pas behind and look ahead to more accurate, engaging, courteous, profes-sional and impressive verbal communications.

A note on the future...

A car has only a small rearview mirror but a large windshield. This is because we are meant to look forward more than we look behind!

"To effectively communicate, we must realize that we are all different in the way we perceive the world and use this understanding as a guide to our communication with others."
Anthony Robbins

Speech

The way in which you speak constitutes 38 percent of how well you communicate with others. It is not simply a matter of possessing a vast vocabulary and a confident approach; it is also important to examine and assess the way your speech sounds.

 How does your voice sound? Record it and play it back a few times—that is what everyone else hears.

"Oratory is the art of making deep noises from the chest sound like important messages from the brain."
H. L. Phillips

Think about all of the different environments in which you speak within a given week. The list below suggests a few of the settings in which speech is used.

One to one with a friend or family member
One to one with a fellow employee
One to one with a supervisor or manager
To an audience (public speaking)
On the telephone
In a group
To children or elders

There are many more situations in life that involve speaking and many require different styles of speech and differing lexicons. Speech patterns differ when speaking to your friend as op-posed to speaking with your boss. Even more evident is the change in people's speech patterns when orating to an audience.

Public speaking is the number one fear among adults.

More people fear public speaking than death!

Do not worry! Nobody is perfect. The good news is that improving speech is not as difficult as you might think. It can be achieved faster than ex-pected. By practicing religiously and disciplining yourself to watch out for mistakes along the way, the journey to better speech will be quick and en-joyable.

Some make a career by talking (I do!), and it is incredibly good fun. When you speak clearly and concisely, your message is more easily under-stood. It is said that when words fail, wars begin, and when wars end, it is words that heal the pain. If this is the case, I think we should all work extremely hard on not letting our words fail us. Imagine how successful you would be if you understood and worked on your speech skills in varying settings. E-mail me, and we will discuss it!

"The art of conversation consists as much in listening politely as in talking agreeably."
Atwell

 Tips

- **Join a local amateur drama club**
- **Read out loud to yourself, and practice speaking—does your voice sound interesting?**
- **Sing (great for a more natural range of speaking tones)**
- **Learn one new word a day (and its meaning), and use it**
- **Join a discussion group**
- **Write some poetry regularly (keep it—you might write enough for a book!)**

Language in the Workplace

Firstly, under no circumstances should you use foul or offensive language whilst in a professional environment, not even with your friends in jest. To do so shows a complete disregard for colleagues and if done in anger also demonstrates a blatant lack of self-control.

The language of a professional should be an example to everyone. Extending your vocabulary and working on your articulation assists in creating coherent and clear communication.

 "I've noticed two things about men who get big salaries. They are almost invariably men who, in conversation or in conference, are adaptable. They quickly get the other fellow's view. They are more eager to do this than to express their own ideas. Also, they state their own point of view convincingly."
John Hallock

May or Can

Being correct with these speech elements will dismiss the need for reclarification, which is both time-consuming and embarrassing. Misuse of may and can should be avoided. Remember that "May I" should be used mostly to ask permission. "Can I" simply asks if you are physically able to do something.

 "The finest language is mostly made up of simple, unimposing words."
George Eliot (1819 - 1880)

Subject Matter

In the workplace, conversational topics should be neutral and business-like. Personal issues and concerns should not be brought into a working environment, as they can disrupt a professional atmosphere and definitely taint your image.   Under no circumstances should personal matters be made vocal.   Always consider your surroundings before deciding on a subject matter for conversation.

"Language is the armory of the human mind, and at once contains the trophies of its past and the weapons of its future conquests."
Samuel Taylor Coleridge (1772 - 1834)

www.linguarama.com/ps/193-2.htm
- Polite usage of language in the workplace.

 Tips

- **Speak more slowly. On the whole, people speak far too quickly and therefore mispronounce words and speak unclearly**
- **Read more and listen to talk radio—it will expand your vocabulary and usage**
- **Choose a week and concentrate every day on every word you say. Is it clear, proper and expressive?**
- **Sound more enthusiastic about things that you want people to listen to**
- **Try to avoid any and all contractions and slang. We have many wonderful words at our disposal. Use as many as you can**

Summary of Element Two

- Just like cars, our own skills need maintenance and repair. Give your knowledge and skills a regular service through further reading and learning
- Focus on your spoken words. Are your messages clear, interesting, and concise?
- Never forget your language in the workplace. It is a special place and deserves special attention to the words and topics used. No lewd or impolite words
- Improve speech by speaking more slowly and carefully and by avoiding slang and contractions

Element Three

Non-Verbal Communications

There are three primary elements which together form communication. Regardless of the situation, the three primary elements act as one to create the way in which humans communicate and the way in which they are seen.

These elements are:

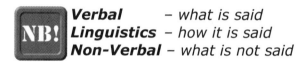

Verbal – *what is said*
Linguistics – *how it is said*
Non-Verbal – *what is not said*

To put these elements into perspective, it is necessary to view the results from a series of experiments by Albert Mehrabian studying the way humans communicate. His conclusions were:

"...The total impact of a message is about 7% verbal (words only) and 38% linguistic (including tone of voice, inflections and other sounds) and 55% non-verbal..."

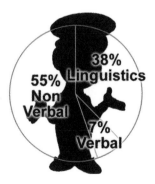

Professor Ray L. Birdwhistell drew similar conclusions through his research in non-verbal communication. He found:

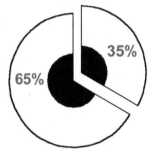

65% of face-to-face
communication
is done non-verbally

"...The verbal component of face-to-face communication is less than 35% verbal and over 65% of communication is done non-verbally..."

These are staggering statistics in favor of an area of communication of which few are aware. Without realizing it, many people have suffered the detrimental effects of poor non-verbal communication. Whether an interview that seemed to go well but instead ended up with rejection, or a negotiation that concluded unfavorably, it is a strong possibility that non-verbal communications have played a large part in these negative results. This section of the book will highlight the major aspects of body language as well as suggest tips for improvement.

What is Body Language?

Body language has only been recognized on a wide public scale since the early 1970s and has yet to be fully developed and researched. Body language is the non-verbal messages we send out. Although someone might not be familiar with the studies and findings of body language research, humans read such signals on a subconscious level. Have you ever met someone and gotten a gut feeling about them? This is your own body language interpreter kicking in. Body language is not just a matter of folded arms or crossed legs; it includes but is not limited to: eye contact, gesticulations, facial expressions, breathing rate, body zoning, and other subtle nuances. It is now considered a tool by the FBI and even used during voire dire by attorneys. Do not underestimate what you are saying when you think you are saying nothing at all.

How Body Language is Read

Body language is usually read and recognized on a subconscious   level. Human minds absorb, assess, and conclude at an incredible speed, a speed faster than your conscious thought, mouth or ears can function. Blinking is a comparable subconscious action. One is only aware of this action once it has happened.

"Words represent your intellect. The sound, gesture, and movement represent your feelings."
Patricia Fripp

In the time it takes for a person to say, "I really am the best candidate for this position," the evaluator's brain will have noted tens of visual images and minutiae. He will have read, assessed, and based conclusions upon them. Before the sentence is finished, the interviewer will have formed a picture, an image, and maybe even a conflicting message concerning the interviewee. This conclusion was no accident. The evaluator's mind took note of posture, positioning of hands and arms, and focus of eyes. He used this information to form the message of what the body rather than the voice was projecting.

In short, in relation to body language, successful communication means that your body signals match and support your verbal messages.

**www.members.aol.com/nonverbal2/
diction1.htm**
- Non-verbal dictionary of gestures and their meanings.

Improving Your Body Language

Make a few simple changes to make your body language support your verbal messages. Although body language is actually a complicated mix of body clusters (meaning groups of individual signs), the following are some simple pointers to get you started:

Look interested
Upper body leaning slightly forward, good eye contact, open arms and hands.

Look approachable and honest
Legs and arms uncrossed, head tilted slightly, un-buttoned jacket or coat.

When listening
Smile, gently nod and use reaffirmatives like "oh yes," "I see," "ohhh," "that's excellent," "I under-stand."

Avoid
Bringing your hands to your face or neck, fidgeting or playing with your keys, pens or coins.

 Tips

- **Talk to yourself in the mirror. How do you look?**
- **Remind yourself in meetings to smile and re-lax**
- **Wear cologne and use breath fresheners (smell is important)**
- **Wear comfortable clothing; if you feel uncomfortable you will look uncomfortable. A few dollars on altering existing clothes can make a big difference**

Summary of Element Three

- The total impact of any message is 7% verbal, 38% linguistic, and 55% non-verbal. It is far more than just the right choice of words!
- Use positive body language to support your verbal messages

Element Four

Written Communications

Your Image Emissary – Correspondence

Letters and the written word can be a very personal form of communication, especially handwritten letters and notes. For this reason, correspondence of any kind constitutes an important part of your image and how people see you.

"If you wish to know the mind of a man, listen to his words."
Chinese Proverb

Personal Correspondence

The handwritten letter is rapidly becoming a rarity. It is for this reason that receiving a letter in a person's handwriting is a special and noteworthy event. You should take advantage of this tool. Indeed, one of my closest friends first impressed me because he would take the time to send out short, personalized, handwritten notes and thank-you letters to his clients and friends.

Consider this: Your boss organizes a meal for you and your colleagues. He has obviously taken the time and made the effort to provide you with a lovely evening. At the end of the meal, you thank him and leave (this is what is expected). Most people do not feel they have to convey their gratitude any further. However, that night, you write a handwritten note thanking your boss for the evening and expressing what an enjoyable time you had. The following day, you approach him to thank him once again and to deliver your note. Imagine what a difference the extra effort on your part has made. This is somewhat due to the power of correspondence.

Correspondence also acts as a perfectly prepared speech on paper. We can spend time on a letter until the message is perfect, then we can deliver it as a flawless oration—something most of us could never do in a live verbal presentation.

The Elements of a Letter

With all this talk about the virtues of letters, I definitely want to take a moment to go over the format of a basic letter.

While I always enjoy getting mail of any kind (please write to me), it amazes me how few business letters are formatted correctly and how many simply don't make sense.

There are many different recognized formats of business letters. Certain companies have even developed their own standards, but regardless of the format, the elements of a letter remain the same.   These elements are essential because without them, the letter will be disorganized and difficult to comprehend.   The elements listed below form a standard recognized as the international correspondence format.

Every business letter should include nine points:

1.   *Sender's Name and Address*
2.   *Date*
3.   *Recipient's Name and Address*
4.   *Salutation*
5.   *Subject Line*
6.   *Body: Part One - Introductory Paragraph*
             Part Two - Main body
             Part Three - Concluding paragraph
7.   *Complimentary ending*
8.   *Signature*
9.   *Name and Title of Sender*

The most important aspect of any correspondence is the planning. You need to know what you want to say (try paraphrasing it into one line), then make sure that this message is very clear. With the subject matter of the letter in place, the completion of each of the nine points is the only task left for the writer. A writer should never produce a piece of correspondence expecting it to be perfect the first time; always anticipate creating at least two draft copies.   Even if the letter looks great and reads well, proofread it several times. A useful proofreading trick is to read the letter backwards or upside-down; this forces you to go through each word, allowing you to find typing errors. Once all the grammatical and structural errors have been edited, print the letter on quality paper and sign it with a quality pen. The letter will now be ready to send. (I did not use this method with this book!!!)

www.swynk.com/friends/janssen/
articles/history_of_email.asp
- A brief article on the history of e-mails.

Electronic Mail

E-mail is rapidly replacing some categories of business (and personal) correspondence. E-mail is a wonderful medium. It promotes the usage of the written word between people, and it's fast. Indeed, convenience is the principal benefit of e-mail, and because of this, we are reluctant to spend too much time on composition. This is where you can set an example of professionalism.

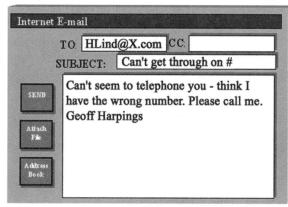

Read these two e-mail examples

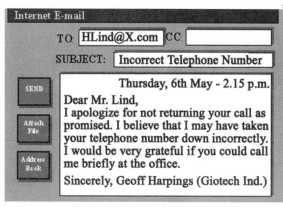

The difference in w r i t i n g time between the

two examples is marginal but with extra thought, the briefest of e-mails can be professional, courteous, and impressive and convey that the sender is as professional.

See how many of my secrets I am sharing with you? Just make sure they stay between the two of us. They really work.

 Tips

- **Be concise, clear, respectful, and positive**
- **Make or purchase some blank cards**
- **Send out at least three handwritten letters and three cards a week to customers, clients, family and friends**
- **Organize your address book into family, friends, and business**
- **For each new person you meet, get a business card or record contact details**

Summary of Element Four

- Most people underestimate the power of correspondence
- Make sure you use the nine elements of a professional letter
- Use handwritten messages on note cards to say thank you to your customers, associates, and friends
- Sign printed or typed letters with a good blue ink pen
- Spend one minute more on every e-mail you send to make it show the professional you are

---

Element Five

Listening Skills

NB! Now that we've talked about verbal, non-verbal, and written communications, I think that it's time we looked at the greatly overlooked, down-trodden, and forgotten ancient art of... *listening*. Listening is more than the ears collecting sound waves and translating them into words. By paying attention with your entire self, you are truly listening.

In order to pay full attention to what is heard, the following should be considered:

> *Voice* -
> *Emotion, tone, inflection, use of pauses, and volume*
>
> *Words Chosen* -
> *Clues as to the attitude and importance of the message being portrayed*
>
> *Speed* -
> *Shows excitement or nervousness*
>
> *Body Language* -
> *Look for non-verbal messages and undertones. You can listen with your eyes*

Research shows that most people will remember only 50 percent of verbal information processed after ten minutes. This means that after attending

50% of a message is lost after just 10 minutes...

After 24 hours, only 10% of a message can be recalled!

a lecture or presentation, you will have forgotten half of what has been said by the time you have driven home.

Furthermore, research indicates that only 10 percent of this information will be recalled 24 hours later.

Consider the amount of information that is lost through poor recall and ultimately poor listening skills.

There are three ways to listen:

Listening Mentally – This includes maintaining concentration and neutrality. Mental listening involves trying to remain a neutral listener and not being swayed or distracted by emotional content. It also involves considering more subtle parts of what is being conveyed through body language and other gestures. Listening mentally is also evaluating when it is appropriate to speak and in which direction the conversation should be led. By considering all non-verbal aspects and weighing them against the real meaning of the words being used, it becomes easier to see what is actually being communicated.

Listening Verbally – This involves two activities. Firstly, it is important to visualize the words and use them to balance the general message. This means creating an equation including the individual choices of words, the meanings of single sentences and the overall meaning of the entire package.   The second part of verbal listening is to question and comment verbally. If what is being said is unclear, it is critical to know how and when to question the speaker. Encouragement and confidence can be instilled by paraphrasing or with questions such as, "What happened next?"

Listening Physically – This element shows the speaker that he is being heard as he witnesses the posture and body language of the listener. All of these positions should be showing attentive inter-est.   Listeners should always face the speaker square on because it shows the courtesy of undi-vided attention.   Listeners should not position themselves too far away and should keep arms and legs uncrossed in order to help the speaker feel at ease. Listeners should also not hold any-thing in their hands to prevent fiddling, which is distracting to both the speaker and the listener. Lastly, listeners should remain relaxed.   Emitting a steady balance will promote a calm speaker. This is especially useful if the speaker is upset.

Listening or Hearing?

"Nature gave us one tongue and two ears so we could hear twice as much as we speak."
Epictetus (c.50—c.125 A.D.)

Listening is a wonderful skill to perfect.   Every snippet of information heard tends to be classified as either significant or insignificant. This classification is directly linked to the amount of information recalled in the short and long term. If our little gray cells don't think that we'll need the information we've just heard, it is sent to the short-term memory junk yard.

In business, good listening skills are vital because you're going to need all the information you can get. A manager who does not listen to his employees may not get the best from them. Similarly, the employee will demonstrate poor performance, regardless of technical or mental ability, if he or she doesn't listen. A person who is a good listener will also seem more approachable, reliable, and knowledgeable because he is recognizing and retaining more information than his peers.

www.adm.uwaterloo.ca/infocs/study/ listening.html
- A study by the University of Waterloo on listening skills. Basic tips and techniques to become a better listener.

"Be a good listener. Your ears will never get you into trouble!"
Frank Tyger

 # Tips

- **When you feel the urge to speak—don't**
- **Repeat what someone says to you to clarify their message**
- **Ask a close friend to tell you a story of their life (a long one), and then retell them what they said. Practice this one often**

- **Ask open-ended questions and listen. You will make lots of new friends**
- **Watch other people; you will learn so much about listening skills**

Summary of Element Five

- You can retain more information if you actively listen
- Visualize the words as you hear them. Try to create a scene of the description to make it more memorable
- Most people remember only 10% of a conversation the next day—if it is important, write it out within the hour

---

Element Six

Etiquette

There was a time when etiquette and deportment were taught from parent to child, but now you're lucky to get eye contact from the clerk as you pay them *your* money. Times have changed. The importance of etiquette has not diminished, but the lessons have.

> *"Parents are usually more careful to bestow knowledge on their children rather than virtue, the art of speaking well rather than doing well; but their manners should be of the greatest concern."*
> **R. Buckminster Fuller (1895 - 1983)**

Etiquette plays the lead role in the show called communication. Without etiquette, there would eventually be a communication meltdown. Consider shopping at a store where employees sneer at customers when asked to assist in finding a product (oh, you've been there too?). What about a clerk who continues conversing with fellow employees or on the telephone while customers attempt to get some help or voice a concern (yes, I have been there too). Without understanding and implementing the basic rules of etiquette, conversing would be too great a discomfort to manage.

www.theworkshoppe.com
- The do's and don'ts of business survival in the workplace.

How Does Etiquette Affect Us?

The rules of etiquette are the conventional requirements for proper behavior on a social and professional level. These standards maintain the stability of interaction and enhance the quality of a relationship through its pleasantries. The areas of communication in which etiquette has an influence are vast. Some examples are listed below:

How Is Etiquette Shown?
Body Language
Facial Expressions
Introductions
Gestures
Listening
Eye Contact
Words
Giving of our time
Tone
Appearance
Actions
Speech & Wording
Attitude

Where Should It Be Shown?
Conventions
Presentations
Social Events
Workplace
Correspondence
In the Street
In the Car

On the Train
On the Telephone
Online Chat Rooms

Remember:
Etiquette is necessary when communicating with anyone at any time.

Simple, Effective Etiquette

These pointers are based on some of the most common uses and misuses I have experienced:

Never discuss personal hygiene and detailed personal health issues with fellow employees. Save it for your doctor!

Never pass judgment on others; it may well be your turn next time.

Be polite. Use: Please. Thank You. Excuse me. May I...?

Help others as much as possible, though not to personal detriment.

Be discrete when correcting or reprimanding a colleague.

Smile. As simple as this may be, it is surprising how many people do not do it!

Exercise common sense. The majority of etiquette blunders are through a lack of this and just plain rudeness.

"Good manners will open doors that the best education cannot."
Clarence Thomas

Time and Etiquette

"Time is money"
Benjamin Franklin (1706 - 1790)

The most important thing to remember about this element of etiquette is to be prompt. In the workplace of today, time really is money. Arriving late for an appointment could be construed as disrespect for the time of others.   Should circumstances delay prompt arrival at a meeting, call to apologize and inform the other party of the new expected arrival time. Handle everyone else's time as you would your boss' new and expensive car–with care!

Conversation

"Two monologues do not make a dialogue."
Jeff Daly

Volume and conciseness are important to bear in mind during conversation, but perhaps the most important element of this area is the subject matter. Everyone has experienced the feeling of embarrassment after saying something unintentionally offensive. These experiences emphasize the value of choosing an appropriate subject for conversation. Always avoid discussing personal matters in the workplace. Apologize immediately if you sense a faux pas.

Professional Etiquette

There are many intricacies of professional etiquette that when combined affect the overall picture of a professional. Peruse the following topics, and think about how each example could benefit the way you project yourself.

"Manners maketh man"
William of Wykeham (1324-1404)

The New Employee

Everyone has experienced the first day at work. When a new employee joins the group, try everything possible to make your first introduction a pleasurable one. Invite him/her to lunch. Take the time to show him/her the building. Simply be nice.

The Company

Progression through any company requires respect. Promotion and recognition are rare for the employee who arrives late, abuses company resources and wastes company time.

"A wise man will make more opportunities than he finds."
Francis Bacon (1561-1626)

Visitors

Be polite and courteous to all those who pass through the workplace. Perhaps invite the visitor to sit and also offer some refreshment. This is the only scenario in which it is correct to give priority to another person over your employer. Good etiquette gives the company a good image which, in turn, builds a professional image for the employee. Being polite to everyone will impress colleagues and supervisors.

www.etiquettehell.com
- A site that describes problems that have occurred due to bad etiquette.

The Telephone

The telephone is a doorway to your company, so it is important to keep the lines clear. Do not take or make personal calls from the workplace. Even if the call is free, the line will not be. Abusing this facility shows disrespect for the company. Keep any and all calls made from a company phone concise. You see, etiquette even extends to making yourself accessible.

Colleagues

Respect is not something that can be demanded; rather it is earned by showing it to others. Having respect for a colleague's feelings, possessions, and space generates a positive working relationship. It is also a part of workplace etiquette.

"*I respect the opinions of others even if I disagree with them.*"
Herbert Henry Lehman (1878 - 1963)

Rank and Etiquette

Etiquette in the workplace requires that employees be polite, courteous, and respectful to coworkers. This rule applies to every member of the company at every level.

 "*How far you go in life depends on your being tender with the young, compassionate with the aged, sympathetic with the striving and tolerant of the weak and strong. Because someday in your life you will have been all of these.*"
George Washington Carver (1864 - 1943)

Relationships

Personal feelings and emotions should not be demonstrated in a working environment. Engaging in a personal relationship with a colleague can be detrimental to your company and can distract the employee from the purpose of being employed – to work. Relationships with clients and customers should also be kept on a strictly professional level.

Should a situation develop in which a customer or colleague expresses personal feelings inappropriate for a professional environment, politely, and firmly express discomfort. Perhaps create a distance from the other party, and be sure to include at least two other people during future encounters.

On the Road

Remember that etiquette can be applied to driving, as well. Whenever possible, try to allow people to turn onto the road from side roads. It is also polite to drive at a safe distance from the car in front so others don't feel pressured or harassed. Whenever someone waits and allows me to leave my driveway or turn onto a road, I always wave thank you. I like to show kindness and help others throughout my journeys; it makes driving so much more enjoyable. Please make my day and let me out.

Employee's Workspace

It is often taken for granted that as relationships develop with fellow employees outside of the workplace, the atmosphere within the workplace may become more relaxed. This is not the case. Maintain professional relations whilst at work, and leave informalities for social situations. One of the first boundaries to be pushed is disrespect for your colleagues' workspaces. Don't get familiar, and never enter another person's workspace unless expressly asked to do so. The same applies when visiting someone in their office. Avoid walking straight into any office or even a cubicle space; knocking and waiting by the door shows respect—even if it is open.

$ As a guide for situations such as this follow the golden rule of etiquette— ***Respect people's feelings and show genuine consideration for them at all times, regardless of who they are.***

Summary of Element Six

- Etiquette sets a professional apart from his peers
- Etiquette should be used in any professional setting
- Keeping people on hold or waiting for meetings with you is a sign of poor etiquette
- Make a strong first impression with proper language, respect, and concern for visitors, first-time customers and new staff / associates
- Drive with etiquette
- Show respect for your colleagues' workspaces

Element Seven

Your Projected Life through the Hourglass

When we are born, only one thing is for certain:
We will surely die, a somber thought and rather
depressing, really. There are those who may argue that death is a wonderful, exciting thing, and
there are others who dread it. Whatever your faith
or beliefs, death is final (at least for your presence
on this earth).

With this agreed, imagine if you will that this time
we have on earth, this time we call our lives, is
visualized as an hourglass. No two people's lives
are identical, no two hourglasses are the same.
Some hourglasses are huge and last a long time,
some are short and quick. None of us knows how
big our hourglass is, but one thing is for certain:
Once they run out, our time is up. There is no ar-
guing and begging for more time or pleading for a
bigger hourglass.   Our hourglass once turned,
once started, cannot be turned again; it   cannot
be restarted. I want you to think about this in reference to how you use your   skills to promote
yourself to the world and also to make you feel a
sense of urgency in your development.

Picture your hourglass. What is inside an hourglass? Sand?

From the moment your life begins, the sand begins trickling slowly and surely, constantly to its depletion. Each moment, second, minute, and day, the sand drops through, never to be recaptured or re-lived.

As the sand trickles down, you lose something from the reserves of your allotted time. The base of the hourglass begins to fill – this base is full of moments of your life: your experiences and your memories. The top of the hourglass is depleting with moments yet to come: your future, your hopes, and your dreams.

NB! With a limited resource, why is it that you often wish it away, waste so much of this precious, irreplaceable commodity? If something is limited and irreplaceable, shouldn't you treat every grain with care and respect? Consider this as you use your time to implement the Projected You.

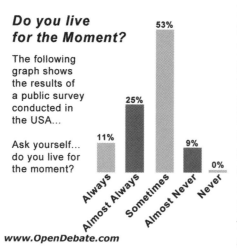

Do you live for the Moment?

The following graph shows the results of a public survey conducted in the USA...

Ask yourself... do you live for the moment?

www.OpenDebate.com

Instead of thinking of your hourglass being filled with sand, perhaps it would be more appropriate to think of it as being filled with diamonds. Or perhaps you should imagine turning the grains of sand as they pass through to the base into precious diamonds. In a similar way, as the Real You passes through to the

Projected You, these elements also should turn into diamonds.

Each day, you should ensure that what is collected in the base of your hourglass is worth something, is not wasted. Time management and organization skills are often taught to better our working practices.   Perhaps you should view such lessons as essential life skills.

Indulge me, and let's analyze your hourglass. It can be broken down into three elements:

- The top
- The middle
- The base

The top –
> *Represents what is yet to come (tomorrow)*
>
> *Work hard to plan goals, and then work to realize them, to make them happen – this is your future.*

The middle –
> *Represents the present (today)*
>
> *This is where you actually live. What is happening to you in the present? What you do here uses up the grains from the top as they pass into the history of the bottom – this is your moment in time.*

The base –
> *This represents your past (yesterday)*
>
> *This is where you will find the irretrievable*

grains. Although used up and never to be re-used, they are extremely important. This is where you can draw upon experience and learn lessons. This is where you can view what has passed. Analyze and utilize – this is who you are and what has made you who you are.

So?

Viewing your life in this way helps you learn the real importance of your life and the real importance of not wasting a moment. Everything you do, every action you take, every goal you undertake will have new meaning when you understand, value, and treasure the preciousness of each moment of your life; the importance of your very existence, your life, your very being takes shape. You can begin to understand that your life really does have value, you start to feel that value and you feel your true worth. You really are priceless.

"Until we can manage TIME, we can manage nothing else."
Peter F. Drucker (1909 -   )

Using Time

Of the three hourglass elements, the most important to consider when seeking improvement is the present. The reason for this priority is easily determined. Since time is not a tangible entity and cannot be altered as a form of measurement, the only aspect that can be altered is the way in which time is filled. The past cannot be changed, and the future remains an unknown in the distance. The present however, is completely in our control. If you change your present, you really can affect your future—now that is powerful stuff!   Thus, people must focus on the present in order to facilitate improvement in their future.

Answer the following questions:

> ·How do you spend your hours, minutes, and seconds?

> ·Do you think you spend your time as productively as possible?

> ·Do you always accomplish what you want to?

> ·Do you ever spend time considering methods to maximize your efficiency?

Time Management

> "If only there were more hours in a day!"

At one time or another, most people have uttered these words. Unfortunately, as wonderful as it would be for this wish to become reality, the measurement of time cannot be altered in any way. Even if it were possible to lengthen the day, without efficient time management, these additional hours would more than likely be filled to the brim with new tasks precipitating the same plea for another increase in daily hours! For this reason, time-management skills are an essential tool for everyone interested in making the most of life.

"Nobody likes to waste their time."
versus
"Nobody likes to waste their life."

Consider for a moment the above comparison. Since time is a measurement of our span on Earth, a logical conclusion would be that when time is wasted, so is a portion of your life. When the concept of time management is approached in this way, it becomes strongly apparent that time should be given the respect and priority it deserves.

This element of **Part 2** will provide a means of assessing time-management skills and will provide useful suggestions for improving individual techniques. At the end of this element, a strong foundation should be constructed for moving forward with a more efficient and productive use of your time.

If money were no object, what would you do with your time?

Travel –	*43%*
Spend more time with family/friends –	*29%*
Pursue artistic endeavors –	*13%*
Volunteer –	*9%*
Make more money for the sport of it—	*4%*

www.monster.com

Remember that   people speak at 200 words per minute while an additional 300 thought-words are being consumed by something else (comments that are not vocalized). This gives rise to the opportunity of multitasking. Multitasking refers to conducting more than one activity at the same time. Such an ability is a talent that, if perfected, can produce swift results which save time and increase productivity.

Multitasking

Multitasking is instinctive. In fact, it may prove more difficult preventing such an activity. Our inherent ability to multitask leads to wandering concentration. There are many different situations in which multitasking is engaged:

·Boiling a pan of water whilst worrying about the dinner burning in the oven

·Driving – changing gears whilst watching the road

·Listening to the radio whilst typing a letter

·Talking on the phone whilst making notes or communicating with others

The benefits of successful multitasking become apparent when the skill is recognized and improved. The following is a basic process for refining multitasking ability:

1. Try to recognize when two activities are being performed at once. Define these tasks and when this multitasking occurs most often.

2. Practice keeping all thoughts and activities on one theme.

3. Allow multitasking while at the same time restricting thoughts and actions to various aspects of the same issue.

Take A Break?

As humans, we have a short attention span; our minds wander, and we get bored easily. To keep your mind on the job, it is important to periodically stimulate the brain away from the task at hand. Breaks are essential to recharge our batteries. We are more productive when we feel refreshed and invigorated. Try the following to assist in this process:

1. If you're feeling unmotivated, take a short break before embarking upon a piece of work. Use this time to take in some fresh air and prepare for the task. The work will not disappear, but taking the time to develop a positive mental attitude toward it will ensure the work produced to be of a higher standard.

2. A small, regular break is advisable and should be taken every two to three hours. This will help to keep a fresh attitude and ensure higher productivity and quality of work. (I always go off and do something creative.)

How To Use A Break

The most important thing to remember is that your break is there to provide a rest for you and moments for you to refresh. If a job demands being at a desk each day, then it is best to leave that desk during a break.   Those professionals working with computers should not turn to the Internet as a form of relaxation.   Breaks should be used to get away from your work station and relax.

Where Should A Break Be Taken?

As a rule, try to always get outside if possible. It is amazing how refreshing it is to see the sun and breathe fresh air after being inside for three to four hours.   Perhaps take a short walk around the building to maintain circulation, or sit on a bench to eat lunch.   However your time is filled, be sure the majority of it is spent in the fresh air.   The benefits will be obvious as this becomes a permanent part of your break time routine.

Tips

- **Keep a detailed log of appointments, leaving at least 15 minutes between back-to-back ones**
- **Before you leave the office each night, tidy your desk**
- **At the end of the day, write a list of things you want to accomplish the next day**
- **On arriving at work, review your to-do list and work through it**
- **Add to it as the day continues so you don't miss calls, etc.**
- **Always have something fun to look forward to, i.e., seeing a friend, going to the movies, etc.**

Summary of Element Seven

- Use the hourglass concept to create a sense of urgency to motivate yourself to use the new skills of the Projected You
- Save time by becoming more organized and by multitasking. It is estimated that up to 25 percent of a person's available work hours are wasted on the change-over period between different tasks
- Complete tasks soon after they are set. The longer they take you to start, the less motivation and focus you will have to complete them efficiently
- Use short, refreshing breaks mid-morning and mid-afternoon to stretch your legs, get some fresh air and relax a little. These 15 minutes will help you to come back to the desk determined

Element Eight

Health

Strength to Persevere

Your body is an amazing machine, truly a remark-able gift. Even as you are reading this page, your body is performing many thankless tasks. Please stop reading for a moment and take time to ap-preciate your heart, lungs, eyes, limbs, and brain. (If they went on strike, what would you do?) A healthy body will serve you well throughout the business day. As your main tool, your body should be maintained carefully. Here are a few ideas:

Sleep

Sleep is an unfortunate but important part of our lives; a tragedy that wastes a third of it. However, this said, I have found that more than two days of minimal sleep will actually take more time to re-coup than you borrowed from it: You will actually be more productive and healthy if you get suffi-cient sleep every single night. If I find a way to escape the "small death," I will be the first to tell you!

·   *A healthy adult will sleep for six to seven hours per night. If you find you need much more than this, then you need to check that you are sleeping peacefully and check your diet.*

·   *Develop a routine to prepare your body for sleep. It is better to encourage sleep rather than to force it. Such a routine will increase the quality of your sleep, and you will awaken more refreshed.*

·   *Try to wake up to a softer noise than that of an alarm clock (perhaps classical music, soft ballads or a natural sounds machine).*

Eating

You must provide your body with the healthy supplements it needs. Vitamins, fresh vegetables, and lots of water are the bare essentials. Sugary snacks, caffeine, fats, and too much of one thing should be avoided. You will feel the benefits of a healthy diet within days of its implementation.

·   *Breakfast is the most important meal because it prepares the body for the day. Breakfast should be light. Fruit, bread, and cereal are sensible choices for breakfast. It also starts your metabolism for the day.*

·   *Lunch should be light. Too much food in the middle of the day may result in sluggish performance during the afternoon.*

·   *Dinner should be eaten before 7 p.m. so that the body may digest the food (and not store calories) before it slows in readiness of sleep.*

Routine

Routines actually help to save you time, maximize your efficiency, and relieve stress. Routines should be developed for the majority of your daily activities. Morning routines are especially important because it is at this time of day when time is most limited. When repetitive activities such as bathing, shaving, and dressing are assigned their spaces within a routine, it becomes easier to find time for additional activities when they present themselves. Our bodies also thrive on routine—sleeping, eating, and even thinking at the same time every day helps our bodies anticipate and assist in those actions.

 Tips

N.B. Please note that you must consult your doctor before undertaking any form of exercise.

- **Have a medical check up**
- **Go walking or jogging and go swimming**
- **Learn through health sites and reading new findings**
- **Take regular breaks**
- **Moderate all you do**
- **Look into the mirror every day and thank your body (sounds crazy but you should appreciate and respect it)**
- **Treat your body like you would an expensive car**
- **Research vitamin and mineral supplements**
- **Avoid skipping meals and too much fast food**
- **As you make an exercise program, also make a sleep program to plan your wind-down routines**

Summary of Element Eight

- A healthy body means a healthy, sharp mind
- Better diet may improve your concentration
- Find more healthy convenience foods
- Consider taking a multivitamin every day
- Spend a few moments to relax before going to bed, avoid smoking and alcohol close to sleeping
- Find a peaceful way to wake up and start the day
- Get a light breakfast every day
- Never eat late—it is bad for your sleep and weight!
- Drink four or more glasses of water in addition to your usual beverages

Element Nine

Assertiveness

Strength of Character

"Dreams are the touchstones of our character."
Henry David Thoreau (1817 - 1862)

Being an assertive person makes a great difference.   It allows you to obtain and achieve things that would usually be expected of more advanced and experienced people. Assertiveness is the confidence that stops professionals from being passed over for a promotion or raise. It also gets your new ideas and projections noticed.

If two people of equal age, experience, good character, and achievement were the only candidates for a position of supervisor, the most assertive of the two would be selected for the promotion.

The following questions will help to determine your attitude when reflecting on the subject of assertiveness.

I am able to easily forward my ideas to my workgroup and managers.
YES   /   NO

I feel that my ideas and suggestions are always given full and proper consideration. They are received with respect.
YES   /   NO

I am able to say "I'm sorry – but no" in response to an unreasonable request without feeling anger or annoyance.
YES   /   NO

I am able to express the problems that I experience from day to day in a reasonable and unemotional way.
YES   /   NO

My requests are usually dealt with quickly and in a professional manner.
YES   /   NO

I have never been blamed (professionally) for something that was not my fault.
YES   /   NO

I am freely able to provide details of my achievements, the areas in which I excel and the achievements of which I am proud upon request.
YES   /   NO

I am always honest in the workplace.
YES   /   NO

Number of 'YES' Answers: _____

7 to 8
You are an assertive person, and projecting yourself positively will be an easy task for you.

5 to 6
You are able to be assertive but could benefit from being more confident at times.

2, 3 or 4
You are rarely assertive - rethink your approach.

0 or 1
You are a wet lettuce leaf! You are probably being over-looked, and your desires and achievements may go un-noticed. Re-read this section.

How to Be More Assertive

"The basic difference between being assertive and being aggressive is how our words and behavior affect the rights and well-being of others."

Sharon Anthony Bower

Until humans have the ability to communicate using telepathy the only way to effectively convey desires and ambitions is through the use of assertiveness. Learning the correct way to be assertive is vital to fulfilling goals and dreams.

A lack of assertiveness can actually do damage. It leads to problems that can slow professional progress. Lacking the confidence to say no or to eliminate problems as they arise has a tendency to cause problems to grow which, in turn, may suddenly demand more time and attention. Consequently, you will have less time and concentration for work while others continue to make progress.

If you don't have the skills to deal with problems quickly, then your professional performance and progression will be slowed.

***www.tsuccess.dircon.co.uk/
assertivenesstraining.htm***
- Techniques on how to apply assertiveness

Achievements

Professionals should be enthusiastic about their accomplishments. They should be proud and let their pride spill over so that others know about it. It is not an easy task because the difference between never promoting yourself and being pretentious is very wide. Somewhere between the two is the ideal balance.

Continual good work may lead to an expectation of those results. Standard and acceptable results in others are seen as poor work in you because the best is what is expected of you. In time, your supervisor may forget your major achievements unless reminded at appropriate points in time. Everyone deserves credit for accomplishments, large or small. Care should be taken not to continuously blow your own trumpet. You may be considered a "moaning minnie" if you go on about how much you do. (Remember moderation in all things?)

"The lady doth protest too much, me-thinks"
Hamlet : III. ii. – William Shakespeare (1564 - 1616)

Make a list of your achievements, splitting them into Business and Personal. Beside each achievement, note two things: which skills were needed to reach the result and when you last talked about this achievement.

Your notes...

Professional Achievements...

_____

_____

_____

_____

_____

_____

_____

Personal Achievements...

_____

_____

_____

_____

_____

_____

_____

_____

What Would Make Most People Happy?

In response to a survey asking what one thing would make them happy, people responded:

I would be most happy if I could...

39%	😊😊😊😊😊	**Get a promotion**
24%	😊😊😊😊	**Spend more time with my family**
19%	😊😊😊	**Change careers**
13%	😊😊	**Make more money**
5%	😊	**Figure out what I want to do**

www.monster.com

Summary of Element Eight

- Don't be afraid to share your views and suggestions, especially during group meetings and idea sessions
- For pay reviews, prepare a small list of your main achievements, successes, and the new skills that you have acquired since the previous review or since you were hired. Submit it several days before your meeting so that it can be reviewed
- Being more assertive gets you noticed—make sure your ideas and comments are positive and useful

- Make regular "Personal Achievement" lists. In-clude any recent successes, i.e., a project com-pleted on time / a successful sale / a new skill / a milestone in your employment history

Part Two Conclusion

Know the elements people are likely to judge you on, and make sure that they include the best you possible.

Some of the items and tips in this section may seem small or insignificant—don't be fooled. As the saying goes, "God is in the details." Pay attention to them as they will say a lot about you; the details will also help to bring about self-improvement and will make getting to know you an even greater joy. Have you ever seen a movie that got better and better the deeper you got? The more your learned of the plot, the more enthralled you were? This should be your character, too: layers of honest, interesting you.

By applying the work you have done on the Real You to the principles and medium of the Projected You, the path to creating your own success will open up.

Part Three

The Perceived You

Overview

In this part...

We all want respect, admiration and recognition from our fellow human beings. Too many of us think we can fake our way to getting it, or simply struggle in the hope that by the end of our careers, we shall be elevated in life through the quantity (years and years) or quality of our work.

A lot of people believe that by simply mastering a (thin) good image, people will automatically like us, envy us, elevate us, and maybe even love us. Something has always puzzled me about this way of thinking. That is that those same people also believe themselves to be perceptive and think they can spot a phony a mile away. Yet when we put our own phony selves in front of people, somehow we believe that we can outsmart them, they can see other peoples phoniness but **we** are coming across as real: They can't tell we're faking it. Know one thing—you can't fake it.

The Real You and Projected You have to be in harmony or else people will see you as a fake—a pretend professional with fabricated skills.

Part Three, the Perceived You, looks briefly at people's differing perceptions and the principle that a combination of projections may create very positive reaction from the majority.

Introduction

The Perceived You is an area that is mostly out of your control. We are merely bystanders when it comes to what others think and feel about us. However, what we can control is the information that people use for their own assessments of us. We can do this by changing what they see and hear.

Once we have a good mix of Real and Projected skills, we can only then apply guesswork to the ways in which other people evaluate and react to such inputs.

"O wad some power the giftie gie us. To see ourselves as ithers see us."
Robert Burns (1759-1796)

(Wouldn't it be great if we could see ourselves as others see us)

The reason for different cultures, fashions, books, music, religion, and the other variants of society is because (surprise, surprise) people are different.

People have widely differing tastes and desires. We all interpret things very differently. This is a positive factor in the development of mankind and has contributed much to the growth of society; discoveries are made because of such diversities of thought. However, when it comes to getting you to be accepted and recognized as successful by the very different-thinking people that make up your world, it can be a difficult task.

If everyone thought the same, I would be able tell you exactly how to act, speak, and dress and provide you a money-back guarantee on near unlimited wealth and / or success. I could guarantee you would be a millionaire in a week (remembering that this would not necessarily be success). However, because people think differently, it is harder than you think. However, grumbling aside, I like the world and the people in it all the more because they do all think differently.

 "Different eyes see different things. Different hearts beat on different strings. But there are times for you and me when all such things agree."
Rush *(music group)*

But many people are not that different at all. Sometimes I give seminars and lectures and am horrified at the lack of individuality in some people. Some are all the same! Same haircuts, same suits, same briefcases, same pens (I actually commented one day that almost all the people had the same make and design of an expensive Swiss pen – is it really that popular?), same handshake (well, they all practiced that from a previous seminar), same job, same church, same life. I so want to grab these people and ask them when they decided they didn't want to be themselves anymore. Furthermore, they are puzzled as to why they

don't seem to get noticed for promotion or reward.

> *"Why do you have to be a nonconformist like*
> *everyone else?"*
> **James Thurber (1894-1961)**

I do believe conforming to a degree is part of successfully belonging to a society. However, let's
look at the "perfect life" that is portrayed so heav-
ily in the media. I do not mean to be cynical here
(but I am about to appear to be, so please prepare yourself).

Success?

You go to school (try and be an honor student so your mom and dad can have a
bumper sticker), you go to high school,
then on to college (you've got to get that
degree to put on your cubicle wall), marry (this is
a must as everyone is getting married, too), have
2.4 children (one boy and one girl is great 'cause
that makes the grandparents happy), don't forget
the dog and cat (got to have one each with ridiculous names). Now, let's see, oh yes, Monday to
Friday, 8-5 work (complain about work load, pressure, and the boss), sex on Friday nights (got to
do your duty regardless), go out on Saturday
nights (it is SO hard to find a babysitter), church
on Sunday (well everyone else will notice you are
there, and woe betide you if you don't go), save
as hard as you can for your kids' college fund (so

they can get their degree to hang on their cubicle wall), look forward to retirement (oh the plans you make: gardening, cooking), holiday once a year (so you can send postcards to prove you got away), retire (so you can garden and cook), have grandchildren (one of each would be nice), and then die (you worked so hard for this moment).

"Life is half spent before one knows what life is."
French Proverb

I do hope you understand what I am trying to say here.

 I am not belittling schooling, marriage, children, vacations, pets, grandchildren, retirement, and death. What I am slamming is the concept that this is all there is to life. I do support and love the concepts of all the above being included in your life, but I am sorry, I do not believe that this is a perfect life or in any way constitutes success.

"Unless you try to do something beyond what you have already mastered you will never grow."
Ronald E. Osborn

So Where is the Living?

What will you say to your maker when you die? What difference did you make with your life? What did you really do with your gift of living? How true were you to your character? Just as clothes do not make a successful person, neither does the "successful life" above. You cannot just put certain things around you and assume they make you successful and fulfilled. It has to come from within you. Your life is your own. In each of us are talents and abilities to share. This is where our success and fulfillment comes from. You have to develop these, share them, and give them to the world. People will see you as interesting, creative, able, and successful (most of the time).

In leaving this introduction behind, I want to share a song with you that has been an illustrative point for me for many years. Your individuality and uniqueness are the keys to attracting interest and enthusiasm for what you can achieve. Or alternatively, you can just be another person living in a little box made of ticky tacky on the hillside.

Little Boxes
Little boxes on the hillside,
Little boxes made of ticky tacky,
Little boxes, little boxes, little boxes all the same.

There's a green one and a pink one,
And a blue one and a yellow one,
And they're all made out of ticky tacky,
And they all look just the same.

And the people in the houses,
All go to university,
And they all get put in boxes,
Little boxes all the same.

And there's doctors and there's lawyers,
And business executives,
And they're all made out of ticky tacky,
And they all look just the same.

And they play on the golf course,
And drink their Martinis dry,
And they all have pretty children,
And the children go to school.

And the children go to summer camp,
And then to university,
And they all get put in boxes,
And they all come out the same.

And the boys go into business,
And marry and raise a family,
And they all get put in boxes,
Little boxes all the same.

There's a green one and a pink one,
And a blue one and a yellow one,
And they're all made out of ticky tacky,
And they all look just the same.

Little Boxes – written by Malvina Reynolds, Ph.D. (1900-1978)

www.bestofbroadside.com/reynolds.htm
- A link to Malvina Reynold's biography

Summary of Introduction

- Don't expect your combination of projections to please everyone—what we're aiming for is pleasing a majority

- You would be surprised at how "individual" you can be and still be accepted
- Don't ever live in little ticky-tacky boxes. What's the point? Your life is a fresh canvas— why would you let anyone else paint on it?

_____

Element One

Commonality of Thought

But if people are so different, how can we influence their perception of the Real You through the Portrayed You?

Here is a little test for you to take. You do not need a pen or paper, you do not need to write anything down. It is a mental test, it is all in your head and needs to be completed with the first things that come to mind (as that is what we are testing). Please do not spend moments mulling over the answer. As quickly as you can, answer in your head the following questions. At the end, concentrate on your answers and then turn the page.

Pick a number between 1 and 10

(Have you done that?)

Now multiply your chosen number by 9

(Ooeer, I can hear those brain cells grinding)

If you have a two digit answer, please add those two digits together (if not don't)

(Example: If your answer is 62, then add 6 and 2 together to get 8, a new single digit)

You have a new single digit? Good

Now subtract 5 from your new number

Now you have a brand new digit

Your new number should be above a letter shown here.

1	2	3	4	5	6	7	8	9
A	**B**	**C**	**D**	**E**	**F**	**G**	**H**	**I**

Now quickly, complete the following three instructions.

Take your letter from below your number and think of a country that begins with that letter.

Take the second letter of your chosen country and choose an animal that begins with that letter.

Think of the color of that animal.

O.K... you should be thinking of a country, an animal and a color. Got it?

Now CONCENTRATE and turn the page...

Wait a minute !!!

There are no GRAY ELEPHANTS in DENMARK

If you didn't cheat and followed instructions properly, you should be claiming I really am a psychic
by now (perhaps I should open a 1-900 premium
telephone line and make my fortune that way).
How was this done? Well, by now you have probably realized that you were poorly led to the answer. True. But, there is more to it than that. The
proceeding mind-reading trick is an example of
"Commonality of Thought."

www.magicandillusion.com
- A fun site with mind games and tricks

Commonality of Thought is the only hope
for us (as Three You's Success Seekers)
and marketing departments alike. People
do think alike (simply diversely within parameters) and so we can use this knowledge to
ensure some of those people accept and utilize us
as the successful people we are. The skills and
suggestions given to you in this book are all
geared to yield positive results with the
"commonality of thought parameters." In general,
people will be positively attracted to people with
strong communication, business, and personal
skills.

We can use this commonality to portray ourselves.
What a clever concept, and it works! People are
different (and here is a nifty secret that makes all

this worth it and should encourage you to forge forward to greater heights), but people do share a commonality of thought. You cannot please all the people all the time, but you can please some of them all the time, and even all of them some of the time.

> *"One half of the world cannot understand the pleasures of the other."*
> **Jane Austen (1775-1817)**

So, fear not, all is not lost. There is hope for you. We will discuss how you can get through to success by following a few simple rules in the Perceived You.

Summary of Element One

- People share a commonality of thought— meaning that in general, certain things mean the same thing to us all. For example, a hardworking, dedicated employee is a plus to all employers.
- The "commonality" example shows us that we can use a certain set of skills and characteristics to please most people, most of the time.

Element Two

The Importance of the Perceived You

The Perceived You is what the world thinks is the Real You. Again (saying it a little louder for those at the back), the Perceived You is what the world thinks is the Real You. This, it could be argued, is more important to your ability to become success-ful in career and life than the Real You itself. This is the concept of the Real You seen by people who control your pay, promotion, happiness, unknown possibilities of chance meetings, and many other factors that will form your future.

"Our self-image strongly held essentially deter-mines what we become."
Maxwell Maltz (1900 - 1976)

While you can never know what people really see when they look at you, you can make some good guesses using the Commonality of Thought. If you haven't realized it, the materials and information found in Part One: the Real You, and Part Two: the Projected You, are your only tools to affect this third and final Perceived You – the one that counts. By implementing some of these skills and attitudes, you can slowly (but very surely) in-crease your probability of success.

"You are only as wise as others perceive you to be."
M. Shawn Cole

It is so important to understand that the Perceived You is assessed by what people (the world) see of you. Because we know there is a Commonality of Thought in motion, we can ensure that the world sees what it likes and therefore accepts what it sees. We can affect the Perceived You through the Projected You and still stay in tune with the Real You. It acts like a filter system (covered in Part 4—don't cheat by looking ahead).

These effects include:

Impressing those around you with your own Real You and individuality encapsulated within the Projected You

Making your character more appealing

Being more original and refreshing

Having strengths based on central parts of your persona that will endure through stress and examination

Having more knowledge

Being able to communicate more fully and on a higher level with everyone

Working more efficiently and effectively

Having a new awareness of what is important to you

Staying focused on your definition of success

Having a new understanding of the people you live, work, and play with

Having a method to translate useful yet generic solutions (found in many other guides and training sessions) so that they apply to you through filtering with the 3Y Filter (found in Part 4)

So the world, although somewhat complicated, has some rhyme and reason to it which you can utilize. You have the challenge to face, but at least you know what you are up against. It is not just a case of dog eat dog; now you can be a trainer of those dogs. You can successfully get in touch with the Real You, present it in a nice package as the Projected You and feel confident it will be accepted as the Perceived You. Sounds simple and it is, but it is a lot of hard work. It cannot be done in a dishonest way; it can only be done if each step is completed in a true and real sense. It is not doing but truly being.

Http://psych.hanover.edu/krantz/sen. tut.html
- Sensation and perception tutorials

"I learned that the only way you are going to get anywhere in life is to work hard at it. Whether you're a musician, a writer, an athlete or a businessman, there is no getting around it. If you do, you'll win - if you don't, you won't."
Bruce Jenner

Summary of Element Two

- The people who control your pay, promotion, and access to the possibilities and attainment in your success blueprint base their decisions on the Perceived You
- Examine which of your facets are seen by people who have power in your life. With your manager or supervisor, for example, what parts of "you" do they actually see the most? Is it when you're working hard? During breaks? By your good reputation? What do they see of the work you produce?

Element Three

Little Hang Tags

Why People Label

 "Labels are for clothes, labels are for tins of food, labels are not for people."
Martina Navrátilová (1956 -   )

It would be lovely if the world were a place where we were not given labels. Sometimes labels seem necessary. At your birth, one of the first things said is, "You have a bouncing boy" or " You have a beautiful girl." From birth we are treated according to our first label. Boys are dressed in blue, and girls are dressed in pink. Not only are we treated a certain way, we are expected to act a certain way, too. This is impressed upon us and reinforced time and time again.

Then the labels increase. "Joey is a gifted child," "Sally is remedial," "Johnny is overweight," "Susie is slim."

There is no way to live life without labels, it seems. Some of them are cruel, others obscene and some are cleverly disguised so as to seem innocent. Understanding why labels are in place goes some way to assuring that you seek the right labels to be attached to you.

Labels are often given for a sense of order. Again, let's look at the moment of birth. The doctor says, "Mr. and Mrs. Jones, as your doctor I am pleased to inform you that you are now the proud parents of a beautiful, healthy baby girl." In reality, there are nine labels in that simple sentence. Let us take them out to show the difference. Imagine if the doctor said at the birth of your child, "You and you over there, as me, I am pleased to inform you that you have successfully delivered this thing." Not quite so nice? And it doesn't really get away from labels. The word label is a synonym of noun. It is just what something is called or how it is described.

Some labels feel good, some do not:

Handsome/Beautiful   *Ugly/Homely*
Intelligent/Smart   *Stupid/Dumb*
Healthy/Fit   *Sickly/Unhealthy*
Hardworking   *Lazy*
Organized   *Messy*
Loving/Caring   *Hateful/Spiteful*
Kind/Generous   *Mean/Tight*
Successful   *Loser*

**www.behavior.net/forums/archives/
gestalt/1998/1_5-131.htm**
- Labels are not for people; only for products

You hope to have the first column used in description of you. However, you should never use any of the words used in the second column when describing anyone else. As harshly as you judge others, you may find what goes around comes around.

Our goal is to get you described in a pleasant way. But the world will pigeonhole you where they feel you fit in best. If you show you are not afraid of work, that you put effort into other people as well as yourself, if you think before you act, and you give to others, perhaps all those kind labels will be applied to you. However, remember you cannot keep all the people happy all of the time.

The Commonality of Thought will prevail here, and people will label you positively if you do the right thing because you feel it is the right thing to do. Always be true to yourself. This is crucial on your path to success.

Summary of Element Three

- Avoid the habit of assigning labels to those around you
- Recognize that labels are very sticky, and people love to stick them. What labels have people already assigned to you? How can you remove the more negative ones?

Element Four

Get Out More

Social Venns

Imagine the world. A huge place full of people. The people gather in various places, and like ever-decreasing circles, it ends with you. The world is split into continents, the regions into countries, the countries into cities, the cities into suburbs, those suburbs into streets, the streets into houses, those houses into families, the families into individuals, and the individual is you.

Within each of the circles, groups gather and sub-divide. Countries make alliances, cities twin with other cities, common faiths join to make congregations. People also create circles of their own: religious groups, political parties, trade unions, special interest groups, hunting clubs, illness sufferers groups, sexual orientation groups. Indeed, there is rarely a topic or subject matter that you cannot find a group established to cover. Surf the Internet, and you will discover that almost every conceivable topic has at least one site dedicated to it. Sometimes when I surf, I am in awe, sometimes puzzled, sometimes appalled, sometimes slightly overwhelmed by what is out there.

I want you now to imagine these groups of people as real circles. Have you ever studied **Venn dia-**

grams in mathematics, where one group overlaps another group in a common area? Now I want you to think of yourself. Which groups do you belong to? Many of us have friends from high school, maybe from college, maybe on the street where we live, and a few at work and church. This really is our world. We minimize our chances of success by minimizing the circles (and scope) in which we live.

If you are to attain success, like marketing a product, you cannot hide your light (you) under a bushel. You have to get out there in the world and let the world see you. What is the point of having a great product (you) that no one

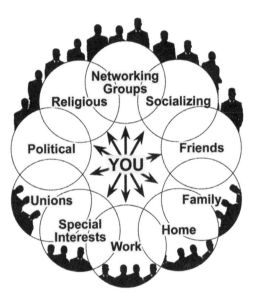

knows about? So, let's examine this. How can you increase your exposure, at what cost, and why should you do it?

"Decide what you want, decide what you are willing to exchange for it. Establish your priorities and go to work."
H. L. Hunt (1889 - 1974)

Increase Your Exposure

Firstly, understand you have something to show. You are as good as the next person, you are as valuable, as talented, and as intelligent. You should look at sharing that talent.

Giving yourself

 I enjoy service groups such as Kiwanis. Joining service groups increases your world as well as helps your community (a must if you want to make a difference – start with your own home before trying to rebuild someone else's). Other service groups can be found in your local telephone directory. I would not even try and list them here. The more you join, the more effort you put in, the better life will be in more senses than one. They are a great place to meet new people, new friends, and new business contacts. You can experience so much when you give. You can learn new talents that you would otherwise not have an opportunity to explore. Pick up the telephone and call a group today.

How often do you perform community service?

16.3%...1-3 times a year
11.6%...3+ times a year
37.2%...Once a month
25.6%...Occasionally
9.3%...Never

www.Kiwanis.org
- International service organization

Discussion Groups

Join a local discussion group. Ask at your library or local bookstore. This gives you a chance to learn and discuss with your contemporaries. It also expands your own personal horizons. You will increase your confidence, aid your speaking abilities and improve your communication skills. It will be fun and informative and something you can look forward to each week. It can be a place to invite your friends and also a place to make new friends.

Hobbies

Take up a hobby or pastime, and work at perfecting it. Join an interest group in your chosen activity. You will be surprised at the number of people with the same likes as you. You can find fellowship and enjoy the company of a supportive, friendly group. If you work hard and excel (as you should do in all things), you can exhibit your talents and even sell some of your work. You could build a website around your hobby. You can personalize gifts to people and build your creativity. Let your imagination go here. You can take up any hobby; what will it be?

Church

Your local church is a good place to meet people,

although please try not to go just to network. Church and religion should be a very personal experience, and you should treat it with respect. Also remember, if you do believe in God, He is watching all of you. Don't use His house as merely a podium for your greatness. It is a place for His. Many churches do a lot of good for their communities and indeed for other causes, so get involved, and make a difference. Let your heart and faith be your guide on which church, if any, you join.

Public Speaking

Start sharing your talents with people by giving speeches and presentations at local organizations. Groups are always looking for speakers. Please start small; it is not as easy as just standing up and talking (I know it looks simple, but I promise you it is not). In other **Xology** books, we spend a lot of time teaching the art of public speaking, so please give it and yourself the respect you deserve by starting out small. You will meet hundreds of new people, and if you work hard at the letters and cards and e-mails, you will keep in touch with them all. Once you have perfected your public speaking, it will increase your personal communication skills, and the world will be your oyster.

"If you're prepared, then you're able to feel confident."
Robert J. Ringer (1930 -   )

Social Events

Go to every social event that you are invited to. They need not be as mind-numbingly hideous as you imagine. You will probably have a good time if you go with a good attitude. Please do not attend in hopes of selling yourself; just be you and hope, at best, to make a few new friends. You could come away with a broader social circle which in turn will invite you to other events. It will turn into ever-increasing circles.

Friends and Family

Take care of your present friends and relatives. Do not overlook them as you are spending more time on other things. If you look after them and care for their well-being and feelings, they will re-ciprocate. Many of the people you know now will still be there when you are successful. They be-came your friend because of your character, without the achievements and successes you are set to achieve.

"Other things may change us, but we start and end with family."
Anthony Brandt

Networking Groups

Join networking groups. These groups normally meet weekly for breakfast and work on referring each other to the circles within other members'

How would you describe your networking philosophy?

48% said...
Schmooze or lose - all of the below

29% said...
Join professional organizations

13% said...
Join others in the industry for lunch or cocktails

9% said...
Join company or industry sports teams

www.monster.com

lives. They are great if you put in what you want to get out – effort. If you work hard to refer other members, they will do the same for you. These groups really do expand your circles and really pay off. Ask around, and get some invites to some meetings. Do not join the first one you go to. Go with your gut feeling, which one feels right, which do you feel you best fit in with, which has the most successful members in its group and why?

At What Cost?

The cost as a dollar amount is minimal for increasing your social circles. The main cost is your time which, as we discussed, is irreplaceable, so make your efforts count. Certain groups may expect a small contribution to their operating costs, but it really is worth it if you make it so. Budget a small amount a month to join various groups and for your hobby. You will be glad you did. It will be money well spent.

Why Should I?

Let us look at your life right now. You have a few groups that you put effort into apart from your friends and family. Maybe one or two circles with little or no overlapping edges. Imagine if you increased those circles dramatically. Imagine if you had 10 or more. Many will overlap. You will be well known, increasing your chances of having your product seen (you) and increasing your chances of becoming more successful and fulfilled.

It really does work. Networking is now a vital tool for successful people (both inside and outside of sales careers), and those who do it right make it to the top of their industry. So, as your industry is "you," let's use networking and your social Venns to get you to the top.

 "Knowing is not enough; we must apply. Willing is not enough; we must do."
Johann Von Goethe (1749 - 1832)

Overexposure

While I am encouraging you to find exposure through networking, I also want to add just a touch of yang in the form of a control warning. As with most things, including yourself, people can be overexposed (and get sick to death) of a product, advertisement, song, situation, or person.

The Carrot Cake Syndrome

When I was only 16, I discovered a new thing. I discovered carrot cake, and I loved it. It was so different from anything I had ever tasted. Each day, I would eat it for lunch, nothing else but carrot cake. Sometimes I would also eat it for breakfast. It seemed I could not get enough of it. I even tried to get various recipes so that I could make it myself and save money in the process. Needless to say, within months, I became sick of carrot cake. I had eaten so much, so often, I became bored with its taste and texture; so bored, in fact, that now I do not even like it at all. I have lost all like for carrot cake. What has this got to do with success?

Imagine owning a chocolate, candy bar, or cookie factory. What do you think your major concern would be? Perhaps it might be theft by consumption, your staff constantly munching on the yummies in front of them. How do you think these factory owners have dealt with this problem? Well, contrary to making the staff wear muzzles, many factories positively encourage new staff members to eat as much as they want. They actually find that after a matter of weeks, staff have eaten so much that they do not want anymore chocolate. What has this got to do with success?

When people find something or someone they like, they want more, and they often overdose on it. They cannot get enough. This is true with many facets of life: employers with employees, partners with each other, pastimes, alcohol, food, diets, exercising, employment, sex, and fantasies.

The truly successful individuals pace themselves. If something is really good, spread it out. Avoid the Carrot Cake Syndrome. Since life is more than one day, it will be there tomorrow. Those who live their lives like there is no tomorrow are living their lives without a future. A futureless life is a life not worth living and one that will not lead to success in any form; it is an empty existence, a waste of being, and a waste of purpose.

"You can have too much of a good thing."
Proverb

You can be very organized with time management, and the Carrot Cake Syndrome can scupper any plans and throw you off target without you even realizing it. Carrot Cake Syndrome can lead to wasted energies and ultimately to nowhere, because once you have had your fill, there is nothing left.

So, how can you avoid the syndrome? Control is so important. A house is built using parts in the right order and in the correct quantities. The bricks are not all piled at the bottom of the house, and then the cement added in a wall above the bricks. The bricks are used with the cement to create a strong, lasting structure. Time is needed for those bonds to grew strong. This is true with your likes and how you spread them out. It is all about balance.

Http://food.epicurious.com
-*This site is just a little bit of fun. Try making your own carrot cake!*

Summary of Element Four

- Examine the circles that you belong to. Consider discussion groups, hobbies, church, speaking to other organizations, social events, friends and family, and networking groups
- Remember that maximizing your exposure through differing circles also maximizes your exposure to opportunity
- Consider joining a service organization. Good things do happen to those who do good
- Do you know anyone who you see too much? Someone that is always around or has something to say? Avoid overexposure if you are already active in several circles

Element Five

World of Standards

As you have read through *Successology*, you may have been familiar with many of the concepts discussed; your familiarity might not, however, mean you are aware of their true importance. We often overlook things because are not sure how to implement them, because we do not have faith in their true value, or we are ignorant to their true importance. Sometimes we reluctantly implement such things because we know we have to; our hearts are not really in it, but it is what we have to do. Sometimes we know that it is important but we simply don't feel we have the time to dedicate to something else in our lives, so we short-change ourselves with a half-hearted attempt.

 "In order to excel, you must be completely dedicated to your chosen sport. You must also be prepared to work hard and be willing to accept destructive criticism. Without 100 percent dedication, you won't be able to do this."
Willie Mays (1931 -   )

The world does not expect to be short changed. The world is unforgiving, and the world expects 100 percent effort and a perfect job well done. When the people who make up the world see and get what they expect, they assign positive labels. This is not a bad thing. To the successful individual, it often acts as a motivational factor and a driving force.

"We judge ourselves by what we feel capable of doing, while others judge us by what we have already done."
Henry Wadsworth Longfellow (1807 - 1882)

Standards are good things. They give a target for the successful person to hit, a goal to exceed. When we meet the standards that the perceiving world sets, we achieve success.

The elements we have discussed within theses pages and the goals that we have set for you to meet are all in keeping with the standards set within the business world. If you meet them, you will be successful. Such goals include (but are not limited to):

> *Communication Skills (including Image)*
> *Faith*
> *Time Management*
> *Knowledge*

NB! By controlling and reaching the standard targets in these areas, the Perceived You will be perfectly balanced with the Real and Projected You's. You will have succeeded in being successful.

What Are Your Standards?

You should have your own personal standards. When you do something, it should not reflect how you personally feel about it. For example: If you dislike speaking to someone, it should not show in your voice, mannerisms or dealings with that person in any shape or form. Everything you do should reflect an attempt for perfection, a 100 percent effort, and full enthusiasm on your part. You may never be able to reach perfection **NB!** in all you do – but your goal is to try. As you grow, you will get better and better and closer to this goal.

Whenever you rush something, whenever you do something half-heartedly, it shows to the world - you are perceived by your results. This becomes the Perceived You. The Real You is a hardworking, honest individual, but because your standards in certain areas are not up to par via your Projected You, the Perceived You is a lazy, unmotivated worker. It is in your best interest to consider and work on your standards. You cannot bluff this; you have to understand, accept, and enjoy the fruits of knowing whatever you do, you do it to the best of your abilities, 100 percent every time.

How About 99.9%?

 If you think that 100 percent (perfection) is a tough order, take a look at what 99.9 percent gets you.

If the world operated at 99.9 percent, then:

- 2,000,000 documents will be lost by the IRS this year. Also, the IRS will incorrectly process 103,260 returns this year.
- In the next 60 minutes, 22,000 checks will be deducted from the wrong bank accounts.
- Every minute, 1,314 telephone calls would be misdirected by telecommunication services.
- Every day, 12 newborns would be given to the wrong parents.
- As many as 268,500 defective tires would be shipped in the next year.
- Two airplane landings daily at O'Hare International Airport would be unsafe.
- In the next hour, 18,322 pieces of mail would be mishandled.
- This year, 291 pacemaker operations would be incorrectly performed.

And...
- 315 entries in Webster's Dictionary will be misspelled.

From an article featured in
"The Working Communicator"
entitled "Strive for Perfection - OR ELSE!"

Make a list of all the things you dislike, the chores that you try to avoid and the people you cannot relate to. Now make a list of what you can do to make such experiences and individuals more enjoyable.

Your notes...

Avoid / Cannot Relate To   More Enjoyable By...

A Master in the Art of Living

"Work and play are words used to describe the same thing under differing conditions."
Mark Twain (1835 - 1910)

Once you have completed and implemented the above task, you are ready to embark on a new journey. The Perceived You will be received with open arms. The world will look at you and not know whether you are working or playing. To the Perceived You, it is one and the same. You put the same effort into everything you do: 100 percent in your work and 100 percent in your play.

Master In The Art Of Living
Scott
(Adapted from a Zen verse)

A master in the art of living
knows little distinction between
work and play, labor and leisure,
mind and body, education and recreation,
love and religion.

He hardly knows which is which.

He simply pursues his vision of excellence
in whatever he does,
leaving others to decide
if he is working or playing.

To him, they are both the same.

Master in the Art of Living is available for download as a
*high quality printable postcard from **Xology.com***

Improving your standards is a living process. Be prepared for lazy days, stop signs, and failures, but good luck. The world is watching; it is what they want and expect of you, a successful person.

Summary of Element Five

- *Both personal and professional standards are important*
- *99.9 percent success and input doesn't cut it!*
- *Be a Master in the Art of Living*

Element Six

Multi-Cultural Perception

As an increasing number of people are working with companies, customers, or colleagues from different cultures, I thought it would also be of benefit to mention the perception of your Projected You by a foreign cultural. A lot of the companies I work with have close ties with overseas enterprises, and even if your company or position does not, I am confident that working with and alongside someone from a very different culture will be a consideration for you soon.

Cultures in the USA

69.1% white
12.1% black
12.5% Hispanic
3.7%   Asian / Pacific Islander
0.7%   American Indian
0.2%   Various

Another 1.6% of the population identified with 2 or more races

US Census Bureau

As so many different cultures would result in different perceptions, I would simply like to offer you some universal guidance for how to investigate and research the relevant parts of a culture.

"Every man's ability may be strengthened or increased by culture."
John Abbott

Researching Your Multi-Cultural Workplace

Thought Method
Consider how the culture collects and evaluates information in the workplace. Many countries have a trend. Some might rely on logic over gut feeling. Others may have an intrinsic need for scientific and factually based information. Knowing these beliefs will help you to do business in a manner that is trusted by any cultural background encountered.

Ethics
Look at the primary ethics and values of the country. Personal ethics may play a very large part in how business is conducted and in how business-people expect to be treated. The generalized principles and beliefs of the country may provide insight into which ethics the person may hold.

"The character ethic, which I believe to be the foundation of success, teaches that there are basic principles of effective living, and that people can only experience true success and enduring happiness as they learn and integrate these principles into their basic character."
Stephen R. Covey (1932 -   )

Protocol and Normal Business Practices
Protocol describes standards such as acceptable greetings and behavior in various situations. Look for marked differences in business procedures in order to adjust to these guidelines.

Language

It is always beneficial to know at least a little of the language. Try to learn something about the language, along with a few words, such as, "Hello," "Good morning/afternoon," "Thank you," and "Goodbye." For the more adventurous, it would be of great advantage to learn such terms as, "It is a pleasure to meet you," or "I hope we may see you again." Any effort made in this area will be noted by the person concerned and will be considered a gesture of good will.

Only one in four Americans say that they can hold a conversation in a second language.

The Gallup Organization

"Those who know nothing of foreign languages, know nothing of their own."
Johann Wolfgang Von Goethe (1749 - 1832)

Communicating with Language Barriers

Speech

Avoid using slang, colloquialisms and difficult words, except perhaps for terms that are industry specific and are probably used worldwide. It should be possible to evaluate a visitor's language abilities fairly quickly. After this determination, an adjustment of speech and language may be appropriate. It is insulting to speak in broken English if the person is fluent. If some help is required, however, consider restricting verb tense and conjunction usage. "Play down" their mistakes, make light of any language problems and be tolerant of small errors.

Non-verbal Gestures

Remember that some non-verbal gestures may convey different messages in different cultures. Be wary of using hand signals before knowing these differences. A good non-verbal communication book or reference will explain exactly which gestures can be used without insult and which will not be understood.

NB!

Did you know that in Australia it is rude to wink at women? Here are some other non-verbal gestures that are unacceptable in some parts of the world:

- In **Brazil**, *touching the lower lid of the right eye means that the listener doubts what you are saying.*
- In **Hong Kong**, *only animals are beckoned with a finger. To signal someone to come to you, reach out, palm down, and flutter your fingers.*
- In **India**, *grasping your ear means either "honesty" or "I'm sorry."*
- In **Korea**, *it is rude to blow your nose in front of people. When speaking to someone, keep your hands in full view. It is rude to keep your hands behind your back or in your pockets.*
- In **Pakistan**, *it is not rude to stare at other people. It is impolite to show the soles of your feet or point a foot while sitting on the floor.*
- In **Sri Lanka**, *moving your head from side to side means yes, and nodding your head up and down means no.*

Almanac

Making It Count

Regardless of culture a first impression is universal. The impression you make is extremely powerful and it is the sum of your image, etiquette, knowledge, personal presentation and communication skills.

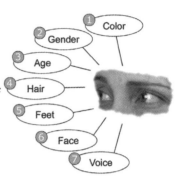

1. Color
2. Gender
3. Age
4. Hair
5. Feet
6. Face
7. Voice

Order we evaluate features of a new acquaintance

In only **4 seconds** someone can make an impression of you that can last up to four years. Imagine what a disadvantage you will be working against in those fours years should that first impression be anything less than impressive.

Summary of Element Six

- You should be mindful of the perception of foreign cultures, as (much to the betterment of our society) we have a varied mix of cultures to work with
- When expecting a foreign visitor, put some effort into learning simple phrases in his or her language. Furthermore, avoid complex words and slang when conversing in English
- Always be ready to make a good first impression. You just can't anticipate when you will make an important first acquaintance

---

Element Seven

The Attitude That You Need

When Business Emotions went on Vacation

Once upon a time, as all good fairy tales begin, in a land not very far away, all the Business Emotions decided to go on a cruise. Everyone who was anyone in Business Emotions was there. Image stood at the front of the line as Professionalism, Communication, and Worry brought up the rear.

Soon the cruise was underway, and all the Emotions started to have a wonderful time. They also started to get to know each other. It wasn't very long before they were far from land and very lost. The captain on this cruise was Indecision.

Suddenly an alarm sounded. The captain shouted over the loud speakers that the ship was sinking and that all the Emotions should abandon ship. Now, Business Emotions are the best at being prepared; they all had their own little lifeboats, and everyone quickly scrambled on them and floated from the sinking cruise ship. Every-one, that is, except for Hard-Work and Optimism.

As soon as they had heard the cap-tain's announcement, Optimism and Hard-Work decided to try and save the ship. After much bailing, puffing and panting, they found themselves in the water - the ship had sunk beneath them. They were terrible swimmers.

Quickly Optimism and Hard-Work called out to their other Business Emotion friends that they were drown-ing and that they were going to die.

Excuse called back that he would love to help them, but……….Excuse's voice faded off.

Blame shouted back to Hard-Work and Optimism that he felt it was their fault the ship had sunk in the first place and refused to help them.

Laziness did not even answer them. He was already asleep.

Procrastination replied that he would come back for them later.

Poor Optimism and Hard-Work were

drowning. Exhausted, they began to sink.

Suddenly they felt a strong hand on each of their collars pulling them out of the water and into a lifeboat. It was Success.

Optimism asked Success why he had come back to save them both. Success smiled, hugged them, and explained to them both that without his two best friends, Optimism and Hard-Work, he would simply cease to exist. He needed them to be Success.

And as all good fairy tales end, the three of them lived happily ever after. As for the other shameless Business Emotions, they all got swallowed by a huge whale called Complacency.

By Scott

"Optimism is the ingredient that makes your work a success."
Anon

Summary of Element Seven

- Success is nothing without optimism and hard work

Part Three Conclusion

It is so easy to spot the people who have mastered the harmony between the Real and Projected. They are "people magnets." Others like to be near them, feel comfortable around them, and success seems to just follow them everywhere. "He seems so comfortable in his skin," "She is just herself the whole time," these are people that we admire, respect and envy. They have discovered a hidden rhythm, and they now seem to be singing to it everyday! They are living their *own* lives, following their *own* goals, and pursuing their *own* dreams.

Our perception of these people is that they know themselves, they project quiet confidence, they have respect for others, and also for themselves. These people were not born this way; they simply realize that they have to know themselves before they know what they want, and they are more happy and confident knowing that they are heading to that destination. They also, more importantly, know that the person they show to the world has to be congruent with their real selves.

Any of us can achieve this end result. All it takes is relevant improvement to our Real and Projected selves, which takes care of the rest.

Part Four

The Science of You

Overview

In this part...

Part Four gives you the basic rules as clear theories. Using theories gives us structure and sometimes clarifies how certain elements interact and affect each other.

Certain elements of this part may be applied to any part of your life. Use the Probability of Success equation to review your progress. Use the 3Y Process to see how the 3Y Theory applies to any situation life presents you with.

Part Four, in closing, leaves you with a more scientific approach and summary to the Science to Success.

Introduction

So far, *Successology* has examined the importance of finding and developing the Real You. Then we saw how using certain skills will assist in projecting the positive and desirable parts to help you to be seen in a new light. The Perceived You is the result of the first two and is somewhat out of your control.

As I mentioned, the Perceived You is also the least tangible of the Three You's as it is based on the opinions of those who surround you, all seeing you at different times, under different circumstances. The people around us will have a range of differing opinions as they, too, have their own colored spectacles, affecting their perception of their world.

However, with such variables and unknowns, it is still possible in this final part to bring the Three You's together in a clear formula, designed to further support our understanding of how the mix of ingredients eventually changes the outcome. In short, while we can control what goes into the blender (Real and Projected You), it is only experience that will tell us that bananas and meatloaf don't go well together (the Perceived You)!

"Experience is the key to greatness."
Arthur Williams

Element One

Success Formula

Let's imagine for a moment that you were a god. (What do you mean you don't have to imagine?) Anyway, as you're looking down, you plan to give life to a very successful individual. Which elements and strengths would ensure, or at least elevate, the possibility for success in that person's endeavors? These very elements are those that should be included in our Success Formula.

When looking at success with a more scientific eye, the components or factors for a "probability of success" equation should include four vital areas of awareness and skill. All four have been covered in the first three parts of *Successology.* However, in this closing part, I would choose to leave you with these four elements ringing in your ears, so that they may be keywords for later reflection, investigation, experimentation, and application.

The primal elements in determining a probability of success are:

1. Time:

As we are all living with the same finite amount of time to achieve our goal of success, those that a) use their allotment to its best and b) have more time to do so will have a better time value for the equation.

This shows us that people who apply their time have more opportunities exposed to them, will continue to grow and will inevitably be spending more time on success-orientated projects.

"I recommend you take care of the minutes: for hours will take care of themselves."
Earl of Chesterfield (1694 - 1773)

2. Knowledge:

Coming in many different brands and strains, intellect is not necessarily the core here. Rather, we need a knowledge of our ourselves, strengths, potential, surrounding opportunities, people, and human nature.

"Nam et ispa scientia potestas est."
Francis Bacon (1561 - 1626)
(Translated - Knowledge itself is power.)

3. Communication:

The single most important skill in life, the foundation of most other skills and strengths and a prerequisite to our pursuit of success, communication is a vital factor to weigh into our success formula.

"Communication is not only the essence of being human, but also a vital property of life."
John A. Piece

4. Faith:

Part Three examined faith and its different applications. While religious faith can be a well of strength, it is also important to remember other forms of faith and belief (faith in a purpose, in a dream or objective). Faith also gives us belief in the existence and attainment of the end result and helps to give us drive.

"Nothing in life is more wonderful than faith - the one great moving force which we can neither weigh in the balance nor test in the crucible."
Sir William Osler (1849 - 1919)

These elements are put into the following formula:

$$Success =$$

$$\underline{Faith \times (Knowledge + Communication)}$$

$$Time$$

Explanation of Formula

Knowledge and communication are our primary elements. They are reliant on each other. Knowledge is useless without the means to convey it, and communication skills alone (although a great benefit for anyone) will not get you very far if you don't have important things to communicate, or the knowledge of how to apply the skill.

Knowledge and communication skills (or K+C) are then multiplied by Faith. The higher the value for faith, the stronger we believe that our goals are attainable, that there is purpose / higher purpose, and that perhaps we are not alone on the journey. This value is also a marker of our resiliency and determination.

Finally F(K+C) is divided by Time. Time is rated inversely, meaning that the more time you waste on non-productive, non-positive, and non-growth items every week, the higher your time value. The higher the value of Time, the smaller the final value for Success potential (or X) becomes. This hypothetical value would really show us our potential of achieving our success.

$$X = \frac{F(K+C)}{T}$$

Evaluating Your Success Equation Integers

Let's find your values and see how this equation applies to you. Find your numbers below, place them into your equation and find your probability of success.

Knowledge:
Place a value on your current knowledge of your-

self, your trade, level of education, and honesty. This is a difficult one, but the previous parts of *Successology* should have prepared you for an honest and rounded appraisal. The more years you have in a professional environment also helps for a higher score in this category. Most people in their twenties and some thirties have an average to good knowledge value, at best.

High Knowledge = 5
High professional / adult life experience. Ability to honestly assess your own desires, faults, and goals. High knowledge of your industry and respect from colleagues for achievement and/or years of service. You have held serious, close, and long-term intimate relationships where little was left unknown between you.

Good Knowledge = 4
Most, but not all of above items. You consider yourself to be a talented and well-balanced person with excellent experience.

Average Knowledge = 3
Most people fall into this category. Average knowledge shows standard education up to and including a college degree, some professional knowledge, and experience and some short to medium-term relationships.

Below Average Knowledge = 2
Limited professional experience in a highly managed environment and mainly short-term, casual relationships and friendships.

Poor Knowledge = 1
Usually adults without higher education, lower motivation, and low exposure to creative positions and roles of responsibility.

My K Value = _____

Communication:
This value assesses your interpersonal human communication skills.

High Communication = 5
Expressive, with management and team-leading experience. Able to motivate, sell new ideas, and nurture a working team spirit. Creative with a penchant for art, writing, literature, or other creative pastimes and hobbies. Moved by sad movies. Experienced in making presentations and some formal speeches. Forward and personable. Good negotiator and peace keeper. Current with topical world, business, local, industry, or sports news. Student of advanced communication guides (Successology doesn't count if it is your first!), seminars, and other company training. Good vocabulary. Applied knowledge of body language, presentation skills, and etiquette.

Good Communication = 4
Most, but not all of the above elements.

Average Communication = 3
Limited public speaking and management experience. Limited creativity and reading. Little or no

sales experience. Not especially inspiring or moti-vating to those around you.

Below Average Communication = 2
Most of average elements.

Poor Communication = 1
Somewhat insular and quiet. Could be described by others as being shy. Little or no experience.

My C Value = _____

Faith

The Faith value tries to determine your personal and religious faith and to which degree your faith positively impacts your lifestyle and character. Also includes your faith in your abilities and in those around you.

High Faith = 5
You put faith not only in a religion but you also make it a part of your life. High faith in self and abilities.

Above Average Faith = 4
You have some religious faith and also apply some of your faith in your daily life.

Average Faith= 3
You have some religious faith but rarely apply any of your beliefs in your daily life. Also have little faith in your own potential and abilities beyond your current skills.

Below Average Faith = 2
Little, or undecided religious faith, with little faith in ever achieving your dreams and desires.

Poor Faith = 1
You have no faith in yourself or a greater purpose other than your own gain. Alternatively, you could also put too much faith into the management of your life, relieving you of any responsibility to put in effort and sacrifice for accomplishments.

My F Value = _____

Time:

Time, as they say, always has the final word. As we are all competing within the same framework and confines, time looks at how this resource is applied in our lives and how much control we wield over it. "You cannot have your cake and eat it too!" – The time you spend on any activity cannot be spent on any other– it is gone. This opportunity-cost shows us the obvious; that time spent on unproductive pastimes cannot be spent on growth, learning, and self-betterment.

Excellent Use of Time: = 1
You are organized and can plan and accomplish tasks swiftly. You are a hard worker and regularly work beyond office hours, on weekends and holidays. You are able to handle multiple projects and switch between them. You also have time for meaningful relationships and learning. You are truly in control of the hourglass.

Good Use of Time = 2
You work hard to minimize the amount of time that each job or project takes. You are known to spend some of your free time on projects, although not regularly. You are able to maintain close relationships with family, partners, and colleagues while still dedicating above average time on professional endeavors.

Average Use of Time = 3
The usual employee falls into this category, producing the expected volume and results, and little more. You look forward to 5 o'clock and occasionally miss meetings and deadlines due to your workload.

Below Average Use of Time = 4
You feel that you are running around at times and that life is slightly ahead of you. You constantly have work to do, letters to write, and old items on your to-do list. You wish there were more hours in the day.

Poor Use of Time = 5
You spend any and all available free time on relaxing, fun, shopping, movies, and non-productive pastimes. You hardly read or use your own time to get ahead with work or develop business, personal ideas.

My T Value = _____

 For a more detailed assessment process of each of these elements, please visit the **Xology** website at ***www.Xology.com***.

My Science of Success Equation:

(Faith) F =	_____
(Knowledge) K =	_____
(Communication) C =	_____
(Time) T =	_____

Now enter your results into the following equation:

Knowledge		_____
Plus	+	
Communication		_____
Equals	=	_____
Multiplied by	x	
Faith		_____
Equals	=	
		_____

Divided by   /

Time   _____

Equals =	_____

 Results

3 & Below   Very Unlikely to Succeed

These are extremely low scores which indicate a very low probability of progression. This score could be generated by a high wastage of available time (a factor that is more easily fixed) or all-around low scores in K, C, and F skills (more difficult to fix). However, you have the most to gain, and some gains will be easy ones and powerful. Use *Successology,* part by part (starting with Real You skills for several months) to improve skills in all Three You's. Start today.

4-8   Unlikely to Succeed

This is an average score. You have an equal chance at progression as others who are not committed to self-improvement. Any progression will be attributed to good luck rather than planned destiny. It is unlikely you will achieve success at this time, should your success-plan include any items that you don't currently have. Any improvements you make from this day forth will put you in above average probability of success. Concentrate on Real You and Projected You skills equally.

9-14   Possible to Succeed

If you have scored in this range, your skills and probability are slightly above average. Your chances are better than even. Use the *Successology* skills with one-third improvement in the Real You skills and two-thirds of your efforts on Projected You.

15-19   Likely to Succeed

Congratulations. This is an excellent rating. Furthermore, your probability will increase by identifying any *Successology* elements that are weak and by strengthening Projected and Perceived areas. It is likely that you will achieve your success plan.

20+   Highly Likely to Succeed

Congratulations. Honest ratings in this range are very seldom. You should arrive at this rating if you consider yourself to be among the country's top 5 percent of the most talented, articulate leaders. Success will surely be yours. If you have not already achieved your success plan, then concentrate a little on Projected skills and consider more social perceptions to ensure your further attainment. Well done.

Element Two

The 3Y Filters

1 + 1 + 1 = 1

In this closing part of *Successology,* I want to provide you with further resources for translating the
Three You's in an applicable process for use in
other parts of your life. Indeed, I strongly advocate using the 3Y process in all your endeavors.
The following element provides a worksheet to assist you in thinking in these terms.

For now, I would like to show that currently some
of your strengths and success factors are not being translated by the Projected You.

As this diagram
shows, the Pro-
jected You acts as a
filter, blocking and
hindering some ele-
ments whilst allow-
ing others to show
through for the
consideration of the
Perceived You. The
goal, as it has been
from the start, is to

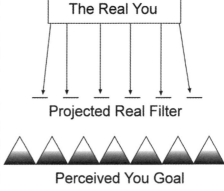

The Real You

Projected Real Filter

Perceived You Goal

facilitate the correct filtering of your success factors through the correct skills so as to strike true

in the Projected You and create a You that is con-
ducive to success.

Through adopt-
ing the skills as
detailed and in-
troduced in the
Real You (from
which everything
stems) through
the changes sug-
gested in Pro-
jected You, we
can re-align the
filters to allow new skills, previously untapped and
unseen talents, individuality, motivation, direction,
and assertiveness to be exposed and do its work.

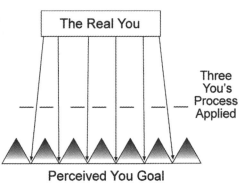

With the correct skills, the Projected You comes
into alignment, and the Perceived You begins to
match.

By matching your three facets you solidify the appearance of your skill, depth, and ingenuity.

Disney Corporation has found success based on
this model. With hindsight, we can see that Disney
managed to align its family qualities with its projected self of the same. As a result, the world saw
and continues to see Disney as a family-orientated
company, and they have found success.

Element Three

The 3Y Process

The 3Y process consists of a formula and work-sheet designed to help you in all your endeavors from this point on.

In your quest for personal success, it is imperative that you leave this book with the determination to do just two things:

One
Implement the skills explained in this guide

Two
Use the 3Y Process to decipher *all* of your personal growth decisions

The 3Y Process will assist you in applying the principles of this book. It will turn your goals into three vital and separate stages and help you to determine suitable changes for the Real, Projected and Perceived You.

The 3Y Breakdown

Y1— represents the Real You

Y2— represents the Projected You

Y3— represents the Perceived You

X— represents your chosen objective

Sample Application

X You want to make a character change in the work place. For this example, we will assume that you want to be more positive. This goal is X.

Y1 stands for your answer to this question: "What does the Real You already do to support the accomplishment of X?"

Situation—I am naturally positive:

Real You—
- *When I am on top of my workload*
- *In the late afternoon (not good in morning)*
- *After a successful project / sale*

Y2 asks how you can use Y1 to show and support X (the goal)

Situation—I can be more active and visible during my positive moments

Projected You—
- *Schedule more important meetings at these times*
- *Make a decided effort to take part in meetings that fall at these times*
- *Participate in after-hours staff social events after the completion of a project / sale*

Y3 is a Perception Statement that explains the effect your **Y2** answers will have...

By keeping any of my natural strengths central to the projected me, people will also perceive me that way. Thus, I will be able to encourage and project select and genuine skills to a specific result.

In this case ...
I will be perceived as being a positive and active part of the company

X *is the goal*

By doing Y1, Y2 & Y3, I will be able to achieve on all levels, most importantly with the Perceived Me, for that is the Real Me that the world knows

3Y Worksheet

Following is a blank worksheet that you may copy and use to explore and translate future challenges and changes so that they may be resolved with the 3Y Process.

3Y Worksheet

X
— What do you want to achieve?

Y1
— What personal trait or skills do I possess that if exposed may help to achieve this perception

Y2
— How can I apply these skills to affect the Projected Me?

Y3
— Perception Statement. What effect will Y2 have on the Perceived Me and bringing about X?

Part Four Conclusion

These formulas can help you see a little more clearly when the elements of self-improvement or the details of our lives become too complex.

Simply remember to ask yourself how the Three Y's apply to your goal.

Also revisit the Success Probability test. If you are able to commit yourself to implement even a few of the many tips and challenges found with *Successology*, then I promise that you will see a difference in your probability rating.

"Success is all around...

Success is ahead of you...

Success is in you.

Find it."

Scott

Xology Guides

exploring

The Science of Living

Bibliography

The following are gratefully recognized as being sources of fact or inspiration for content, statistics, reference, language, and terminology as appears in Successology:

Time Almanac 2001
U.S. Census Bureau
Yahoo.com
Monster.com
American Demographics
"Fast Food Nation" - by Eric Schlosser
"Overweight" – An article by Martha Brassil, B.A., D.Th.Dip.
www.urbaninstitute.org - The Urban Institute
www.uli.com - Urban Land Institute
OpenDebate.com
US Department of Education
Communications and Business Integration Course Material
Fedstats.gov
Fitness Magazine
"Aristotle" - by Kenneth McLeish
The New York Times
Info Please Almanac
Webster's Dictionary
Baylor College of Medicine
Encarta, by Microsoft
Aol.com
Time Magazine
Washingtonpost.com
Compton's Encyclopedia
Encyclopedia Britannica
Encyclopedia.com
Stanford Encyclopedia of Philosophy—Http;//plato.stanford.edu
The Bible - King James Version
World Almanac
Gallup Organization
The Wall Street Journal
"Universe" - by Stephen W. Hawking
"Plato" - by Bernard Williams

The Author

Scott Rogers

Scott Rogers enjoys his life solving problems and making companies successful.
Scott is among a select group of the most
admired and respected business experts,
speakers and facilitators. Scott has worked for over 10 years
on nearly every continent working with many thousands of
people. He shares his vision and skills through training
events, consulting, and executive one-on-one sessions.
'Successology' is Scott's first self-help guide which departs
just some of the knowledge he has gathered and developed
during his career.

"This man can truly be considered the 'guru' and oracle of his field"
Dr. C. Warner, Editor—Business State Magazine

Scott is an award winning keynote speaker on many business
issues and advanced personal skills. Scott's original and ex-
hilarating sessions are acclaimed and recommended by nu-
merous national organizations and are also hailed as being
among the country's best by businesses and attendees alike.

On a lighter note, Scott is the #1 fan of The Simpsons show
and SpongeBob SquarePants - with hair equally to match!

Speaking Engagements
Scott is available for engagements for your business, association, and industry. Please contact 1stCo at **Speakers@1stCo
.com** with your event and training needs.

Contact the Author:
Contact Scott with your thoughts, stories, successes, comments, and ideas. E-mail: **Scott@1stCo.com**

Other Titles By The Author:
Opinionated!   *A book of probing questions for discussion*
Opinionated! II   *More probing questions with Ammo-Facts*
Lifeology   *The Science of Living—the second 'ology' title*
Also the author of a best-selling children's series

The Editor

Mindy Brodhead Averitt

Mindy Brodhead Averitt began her career as a feature writer for the *Baton Rouge Morning Advocate*. She has served as the editor of a parenting publication, community newspaper, and industrial magazine. Her work has appeared in local and regional publications across the country.

She is the co-author of Sacked: The Dark Side of Sports at Louisiana State University and is currently writing the history of a local hospital. She hosts a radio talk show for the Louisiana Children's Trust Fund.

An honors graduate of Wake Forest University, Averitt lives in Baton Rouge, LA., with her husband.

The Xology Series.

Development Guides with a Difference.

Welcome to *Successology*, an **Xology**: Science of Life guide.

Xology Guides are written to provide you with real tools and real possibilities. The books in this series, starting with *Successology*: The Science of Success, provide topics and goals and are designed to act as your personal coach; to encourage, guide, correct, and succeed with you.

Along with the purchase of any **Xology** title comes access to further reference materials and personalized utilities on the Xology website.

Make sure you visit **www.Xology.com** to benefit from useful features such as the *Successology*: *Success Schedule* online program - a web-based application that will track your progress, encourage you to examine your successes and failures, and report on your achievements.

Xology Guides can be relied upon for clear direction, new thinking, and a dedication to your success in life.

Rely on forthcoming *Xology Guides* for your pathway to Success, Sales, Communication Skills, Motivation, Life and more.

Xology was created to provide professional and intelligent guides to important elements of our everyday lives.

Designed to be more engaging than other brightly colored guides, and more accessible than exhaustive business volumes, *Xology* is for your life.

Xology Guides

exploring

The Science of Living